FEATHERS FROM THE ANGEL'S WING

# FEATHERS FROM

# THE ANGEL'S WING

POEMS INSPIRED BY THE PAINTINGS OF
PIERO DELLA FRANCESCA

EDITED, WITH AN INTRODUCTION BY DANA PRESCOTT
FOREWORD BY ROSANNA WARREN

A KAREN & MICHAEL BRAZILLER BOOK
PERSEA BOOKS / NEW YORK

Persea Books, Inc.
277 Broadway
New York, NY 10007

Library of Congress Cataloging-in-Publication Data
Feather from the angel's wing : poems inspired by the paintings of Piero Del la
Francesca / edited by Dana Prescott ; foreword by Rosanna Warren.—First edition.
        pages cm "A Karen & Michael Braziller book."
Includes bibliographical references.
ISBN 978-0-89255-468-3 (hardcover : alk. paper)
1. Art—Poetry. 2. Poetry—21st century. 3. Piero, della Francesca, 1416-?–1492—
Influence. I. Prescott, Dana, 1952– II. Warren, Rosanna.
PN6110.A77F43 2016
808.81'9357—dc23
                2015028917

First edition
Printed in Malaysia
Designed by Rita Lascaro

For my family

# CONTENTS

## MILANO

## URBINO

## THE PIERO TRAIL & OTHER THOUGHTS

# FOREWORD

Poets are startled by Piero della Francesca, wounded by him, compelled and mesmerized. These reactions are all, perhaps, versions of falling in love. The poems collected here are as various as the ways of love, and their variety, far from exhausting or even clarifying the subject, points ever more poignantly to the mystery of Piero's paintings.

Piero strikes nearly impossible balances and establishes precarious harmonies. His people seem majestic, hieratic, idealized; yet they are individuals caught in particular dramas, like the severe angel with kohl-ringed eyes standing behind the Madonna in the Madonna di Senigallia, or the tired soldier guarding the sleeping emperor in torchlight in The Dream of Constantine. Piero's world seems oddly frozen, yet in it horses trot and rear, banners swirl, and drapery falls in noble pleats. Humans appear otherworldly while angels obey the laws of gravity. The landscapes—the almost bare, olive green hills, the toy towns—tilt so close we could reach out and touch them, but the drawing tells us that they lie miles away. The light seems eternal, yet farmhouses, trees, and white ducks are scrupulously reflected in the river, and sunlight falls at a believable angle through window panes to design a parallelogram on the wall, and to model the entranced but solid bodies of mortals and angels.

Are his people sleepwalking? Are they under a spell? Their eyes may be open but it's as if they've been hypnotized. They could have stepped from the fields around Borgo San Sepolcro but they've been enchanted: conscripted into dramas larger than themselves, they rise into the dignity of their occasions—to give birth to God, to foresee Crucifixion, to rise from the tomb, to march in an army of faith. Their costumes testify to the grave simplicity of their roles: bold, harmonious, monochrome garments whose wearers act their parts in a larger design.

The poets respond in varying measure to the mixture of earthly and unearthly in Piero. Albert Goldbarth, in "1400," a poem of one long, driving sentence, tracks an Incarnation in reverse, unreeling the list of mucky materials—"saps, and the anal grease of an otter, and pig's blood" and so forth for twenty-five lines—that were scraped, boiled, and pounded into pigment in which the ethereal reality would take shape. Others concentrate on geometry, that elemental language of ideal forms with which Piero built his worlds. Judith Baumel, in "World without End," sees in the pregnant belly of the *Madonna del Parto* of Monterchi the roundness of the earth that "confounded" Columbus in 1492, the year of the painter's death: "a slit of white underdress covers a belly/ expectant, low and round like the globe."

This painting has given birth to many poems. Part of its power, no doubt, rises from its placement. In the old days, when I first saw it, you had to take a pilgrimage to find it, driving through the Umbrian hills, pastures, and tilled fields to reach the farmyard and adjoining chapel which housed the treasure. You had to locate the guard, negotiate for the key. Eventually, if you were lucky, the door would be opened. It opened upon a painting about majestic openings, a theater of openings from this world into eternity. As the guard pushed wide the chapel door, two angels thrust aside the tapestried side flaps of a tent, revealing the Madonna, an axis mundi of sober fertility, whose delicate right hand, in turn, coaxes open the folds of her robes from her swollen womb. A great play is about to begin.

These days, the painting is up the road in a glass box in an old schoolhouse. Still visible. Still opening. But wherever one found it, in farmyard, church, or museum, the Madonna del Parto would have the force of revelation. It has troubled poets. Gabriel Fried, in "The Majesty of Piero della Francesca," confesses himself ecstatic at "the long fingers of her right/ hand already spreading the unfastened lips of fabric," but ponders whether he, as a viewer, and a Jew, has been included in or excluded from the sacred invitation. Jorie Graham, in "San Sepolcro," one of her best known poems, presses hard upon the preposition "in" and the verb "to go" : "to go into// labor. Come, we can go in . . . " She leads us further and further into the "privacy" of an as-yet-unborn tragedy. Like Fried, Karl Kirchwey in "Madonna del Parto" weighs the possibility that the angels are not opening the tent, but closing it: "Or do they raise them, in their mercy,/ That we might apprehend celestial love?" One senses, in all these poems, the shock of seeing. "So what is beauty?" Mark Wunderlich is provoked to ask in "Speak, Blood," another poem stirred into being by the Madonna del Parto. Charles Wright, for whom Italy has been a life-long revelation, feels in the Piero landscape in "Umbrian Dreams" "as though a wound, somewhere and luminous/ Flickered and went out,/ Flickered and went back out—/So weightless the light, so stretched and pained . . . " Piero confronts the viewer with a world so fully realized, so solemn, so stark in its power, it can knock you off balance. Perhaps it's because Piero's balance is so much greater than ours; so much is at play within his frames. The poems register that shock. Kirchwey starts "A Limbo of Vanity" by declaring, "My life's so dark I must cover my eyes." Gjertrud Schnackenberg, in "Soldier Asleep at the Tomb," displaces the shock onto the condition of the fresco, *The Resurrection of Christ:* " . . . There is a plaster crack/ Ascending through the air/ Above your head . . . ," a crack that will spread figuratively through this long poem to threaten the Roman Empire and break the barrier between earth and heaven.

Henri Cole is no stranger to shocks. His sonnet "The Flagellation" —in its almost brutal, down-to-earth directness—goes to the heart of the matter, the sense of incompatible realities being forced into a unified composition. Piero's paintings tell stories of human suffering magnified, of people mobilized into myth. Cole ends his poem with a vision of Christ being whipped, but that assault has been subtly assimilated to the speaker, whose "eyes drift back/ To the deviant, the melancholic, the real, emotion/ Punching through the rational..." The bold last line might describe, as well, the experience of a viewer of Piero's paintings, a viewer brought willy-nilly into another state, "As a man for his beliefs receives blow after blow."

The reader will find here many Pieros to which poets have responded, a tribute to the Master's infinitely suggestive power, and to the responsiveness of modern viewers who have allowed themselves to by lured out of their own era into timeless vision. The painter of the *Madonna del Parto* has opened the way for many births, not least among them the fertility of this radiant collection.

—Rosanna Warren

# INTRODUCTION

For years I have taken students, colleagues, friends, family, fellow artists, and writers along a breathtaking route through Tuscany, Umbria, and the Marche—known affectionately and reverently as the Piero trail—to see the works of Piero della Francesca, the illustrious and beloved Renaissance painter, who was born and died in the small walled city of Sansepolcro, about 65 kilometers from my Italian home.

The countryside itself prepares us for our viewings of the art ahead: the narrow, bumpy roads bisecting the immaculately cultivated fields of winter wheat, corn, tobacco, grapes, poppies, and sunflowers. Terraces of fruit trees rise from either side. We come across herds of sheep, tractors, raptors, pheasants, trucks of pigs or cows, and stacked-up cylinders of hay. Laundry on clothes lines snaps in a stiff breeze, hangs heavy from rain, or stiffens in the hot sun, depending on the season.

The landscape of our pilgrimage is the living landscape we see, replicated in subtle pigments, in Piero's paintings, rising behind his annunciation angels and praying Madonnas; it is (minus the tractors and motor cycles) the landscape of Piero's childhood, and it informs and infuses every painting and project he undertook. Piero's paintings are about divine subjects very much anchored in the real world. We see saints, members of the holy family, apostles, all placed near stucco houses or under cypress trees. Heavenly questions are pondered by figures who look very much like the farmers whose fields we pass. The celestial is brought to earth through Piero's absorption in what surrounded him in his everyday life. To rush through the journey, even if it were possible, would mean arriving unprepared for the images that Piero painted. We are somehow more receptive to the subdued colors, the quiet settings, and the peaceful, unmoving clouds, because we have traveled through the very spaces he inhabited.

In our twenty-first-century lives, we are bombarded by visual stimulation; even when our aim is to view art, we see the works crammed together in blockbuster exhibitions or in images flashed across computer screens. To gaze at one masterpiece at a time, isolated in its own setting, not far from or exactly where it was made, is an entirely different experience.

One day, many years ago, I made an unexpected and delightful discovery: a poem by Judith Baumel about Piero's *Madonna della Parto*, in which a childlike Mary is depicted just before giving birth to her son. This painting is located in Monterchi, the Tuscan hill town where Piero's mother was born. It has always been a favorite of mine, especially moving because it is still regarded as a precious relic, one believed to insure safe passage through childbirth. (At the youthful Madonna's feet, below the painting, present-day pilgrims deposit flowers, notes, pleas, prayers, and letters of thanks.) I copied Baumel's poem, and took it along on my next trip to see the Pieros. I read it out loud to a group of scruffy art students standing opposite Mary's "single maternal / face of fear, peace, desperation, patience, exhaustion." More accustomed to a fast fix, the students slowed down, listened, absorbed, and sketched, seeing with a writer's eye "the bursting drapery of her blue dress, / a slit of white underdress covers a belly / expectant, low and round like the globe."

Baumel's work was just the first poem that I discovered in response to Piero's paintings. Many others had been moved to write: Next I discovered the American poets Jorie Graham and Gjertrud Schnackenberg. Then I came across Pier Paolo Pasolini's poem about *The Story of the True Cross*, a series of frescoes in the church of San Francesco in Arezzo. Through these writers' work, I found good company for my musings on Piero.

Something in the works of Piero leaves room for a poet's or a viewer's imagination. Maybe it's the mix of daily life merged with the divine. The works give unusual access, in this way, to the celestial realm, to mystery, to the unknowable. The transcendent. Maybe the inspiration comes from the ambiguity of a downcast glance or the clarity of mathematical precision, or how a limited palette involves the observer through a chalky mars-red, a faded grey green, and a startling blue. The uncanny intensity of an angel's stare burns into our memory. Time stands still in Piero's work; not even the clouds or the stars move. And perhaps this stillness calls upon us to be watchful, receptive, and nudges a poet's imagination to move and come to life.

In 2007, I became director of Civitella Ranieri, an international artists' haven outside of the small town of Umbertide, and not too far from Piero's home in Sansepolcro. These years continue to be the most wonderful of my life's work in education and the arts. I live within a half hour's drive of Piero's greatest masterpieces; and, often, with my resident Fellows, I venture forth to see the work in town halls and churches and small museums. I select poems to accompany us; I staple them together, and off we go. Often we read the poems aloud on site as the voices of these poems are such good companions to Piero's work. Some basic art historical information is, of course, essential to set the context and the history, but any guidebook can supply *that*. What works better, to my mind, as a companion and guide to the art are these very poems collected in this volume.

In choosing the poems for this anthology I looked for qualities akin to Piero's work: a strong sense of craftsmanship, simplicity, and a kind of—for lack of a better word—reverence. I looked for integrity in the writer's thoughts. I looked for something to move me, even if I didn't always understand why, something that communicated beyond the subject of the poem to some larger world of ideas. I like the elegance of many of these poems and the hunger of the writers to grapple with the unresolvable ambiguities of Piero's paintings.

I like to think of this book, organized by the towns where the paintings are found, in your hands on your travels to Italian hill towns. I like to think of you standing in churches, reading the poems *sotto voce* to the company you've brought along for the sojourn to the mountainous region of middle Italy, as you stand in front of Piero's sacred and mysterious worlds. My best advice is to go slow, see one or two things a day. And right there in front of the images, or at a café afterward, read the poems again. Reading poetry while looking at paintings is a pleasure, once you start. To see something in real time, in real life, and not in reproduction, lends authenticity to the experience of travel. It is my hope that the poems in this anthology will help prolong the pleasure of travel, and of engagement with the work of Picro della Francesca.

Dana Prescott
Gubbio, 2015

MILANO

MARE
ADRIATICO

URBINO

SANSEPOLCRO

AREZZO

MONTERCHI

N

PERUGIA

The Piero Trail

FEATHERS FROM THE ANGEL'S WING

MONTERCHI

Friends say: well, you've been there and seen a lot; you liked Duccio, the Dorian columns, the stained glass at Chartres and the Lascaux bulls-but tell us what you've chosen for yourself; who is the painter closest to your heart, the one you'd never exchange. A reasonable question since every love, if true, should efface the previous one, should enter, overwhelm and demand exclusiveness. So I pause, and reply: Piero della Francesca. —ZBIGNIEW HERBERT

[Piero's paintings] are like acts of charity,
and more: they contribute to the general good.
—MARILYN LAVIN

*Madonna del Parto (The Pregnant Madonna)*

## Judith Baumel
# WORLD WITHOUT END

If you believe the various records and registers,
on the very morning that the Genoese, in the commission
of King Ferdinand and Queen Isabella of Castile, set
foot on the island of Guanahani–San Salvador–Watling,
Piero della Francesca died at the Via Aggiunti,
in the town of his birth, Borgo Sansepolcro.
If you believe Vasari he was blind. The works
lead us to believe that this Euclidean scholar's
round-bellied women turned finally,
in the "Madonna of the Birth,"
into a sort of Riemannian proposition of beauty.
That enormous-bellied woman in Monterchi
may have been homage to Piero's own mother,
called Francesca or Romana, depending
on whom you believe. And she may have been
buried in the adjoining graveyard the year before
Piero drew the curtains open, held by his familiars,
his constant angels draped in red and green
with alternating, matching socks and wings.
They present one more enigma of Piero—
this utterly peculiar image, a single maternal face
of fear, peace, desperation, patience, exhaustion.
Beneath the bursting drapery of her blue dress,
a slit of white underdress covers a belly
expectant, low and round like the globe.
I believe the third Book of the Dead
of the Confraternity of San Benedetto,
which registers the end on 12 October 1492, and
I believe he left this world in peace at the very moment
that Columbus was confounded by the roundness of the earth.

And so believe that the master of perspective
closed his part of the Renaissance, a birth
in the Old World and a life that so loved
the even older East of Constantinople,
by ceding spirit to the new one, mother
of all manner of strange round fruit,
its baskets of tomatoes, corn kernels, potatoes,
and to what was being born there, a new form of innocence,
three dimensions of roundness where everything converges
without parallel lines. And where the son of my
future was, remains, and becomes a mystery of flesh.

Jorge Esquinca
NOSTALGHIA

1
I speak to you, Lady,
in words of my time
still new as the boy's laughter
as he cut this morning's bread.
You sway a little, in the soft
shadows where you dwell,
like a boat painted
inexpressibly blue.
To speak of that blue
I would have to compare it
to a sea I haven't seen
or to a distant heaven,
sea and heaven entwined
in feminine conjugation.
To say, for instance,
"there was lapis lazuli in it"—
such words won't do,
beautiful as they are.
Words are not bridges
as we sometimes believe
but guardians of gates.
They rise up between us and things
like the twin angels
that open/close,
as if flustered for a moment,
the curtain of your Mystery.
Wingèd creatures—powerful,
yes, but not of themselves.
Always the core

of their strength
lies in a dimension apart,
impalpable, not human.
Yet what I vaguely
call "not human"
urges, insists, summons us
from its dark Origin.
Words inhabit us.
They enter us and depart
without our knowing for sure
where they come from.
They are *terra verde*, yes, but
blood and bone and muscle, too,
and something lighter, air.
Our connection is made
of an endlessly rocking motion.
Between what's seen and what's gone,
one form to another,
the substance of what we are
and do not know becomes incarnate
and takes breath. Later it comes
undone, perhaps too soon. Blade
of grass, *straw of the world*,
we slip away
like the outline of a bird in mist.
Not knowing whence
or where.
There you stand, pregnant child,
in your silence—*gravitas*,
enclosed in your own gravid state,
as if it were nothing,
as if it were everything.

2
Flower inside the flower,
ark within the ark.
Your hands in the customary pose
of one bearing in her womb
the weight of new life.
Above the long armhole
just where it bulges
your right hand lies open
like a snowflake or petal.
The left hand leans, graceful,
at your weary waist.
I can barely see your feet
that hold you erect
and proud, with the simple charm
of that other girl-child
who carried the world in her womb
as she took shelter from the rain
in the doorways of Mexico City.

3
Over the years,
lulled by joy
or afflicted with grief,
I've won and lost a kingdom,
only to learn that nothing
is ever ours but the darkness
where we make our way. This cheers us on
because darkness itself is nourishment
and your image, Lady, your little brightness,
has comforted me since I can remember
and even before that.

I grew up beside your
endlessly swaying lamp,
and the fuel that sustained the boy's
blind faith ran out, but not your light.
*I have been told to reason by the heart,*
*but heart, like head, leads helplessly.*
Even so I have inherited
a strange protection,
never gratefully enough.
*Bona Dea*, steady vessel
in an uncertain sea,
I received, unquestioning,
your mysterious gift. I attest to it here.

4
Your hair is gathered up
into a knitted scarf
and your head, pale flame
from an unseen wick,
gives off a light, *that light.*
Noble archway,
your brows barely drawn,
your eyelids softly closing,
call us to gaze into your gaze.
Eyes turned inward,
eyes of one awaiting what she knows,
immersed now in time,
bearer of *the spiritus mundi,*
world sorrow—
child, yourself the fruit of the Word,
you carry in your womb that fruit,
that Word.

Cloud inside the cloud.
Droplet enclosed in another drop.
You flow in the spring
that bursts from you. You open
a space for the future word that
already names you, and in that act
gives us a name, a reason
for being, perhaps, a fortune, or rather,
an abyss. But these mirror-image
angels—are they opening or closing?
When we gaze, they gaze back.
Saying nothing. They come, distant as I,
from the mystery they protect.
In your secret kernel, Lady, nothing
happens; everything *is*. And is
infinitely being. Even now.
The miracle birth, the visit
of the Magi, the flight
into an Egypt I live in
when I dream. The son walking
on water. You are that water,
that cross and crown of thorns,
you the selfsame cautery and flame,
substance that gives life to these words.

5

I turn my eyes away. Do I close them?
Once again I behold the splendor
I found in Prague one night.
It was your voice. A gentle thunder,
the Rain speaking within the rain.
Pregnant child, I have seen you take shelter,

frightened and stiff with cold, beneath
a great tree in Oaxaca.
                        So today, as before,
you are the face I saw in the holy card—
schoolboy in flight,
an orphan, though not,
tied to the yoke of a desk in school.
I turn my eyes away. Do I open them?
Here you stand, in the tiny room
of the museum in Monterchi. Before,
you watched over souls in a graveyard,
survived two earthquakes, two wars,
unharmed and blue.
Outside, it's the tenacious Tuscan summer,
sunflowers aflame,
prolonging a late afternoon
of heightened shadows.
You gravitate in this space
with perfect *gravitas,* in this arch
of Piero, in the pomegranate flower,
the heaven, perhaps, of an image
only visible in stillness,
steadfast maker of peace.
The world is green earth, earth
transfigured in words
that never manage to hold
all human emotion.
These words, Lady, say something of
the dream cut short by morning, the dream
sown without knowing in the night.

*Envoi*
But did you truly know?
*Ecce Ancilla Domini,* you meekly answered
the greeting of a Messenger
more startled than you, who'd come
in a maelstrom of voices.
Queen and handmaid, brief abode
of the eternity awaiting you.
According to your will, you said,
in a voice already containing what
would ask for the first miracle.
If I am anyone, I'm the prodigal son
of that voice I have seemed at times
to hear in the wind or water of dreams.
Your dear servant, your runaway deer,
I have attempted it here and now:
by the light and shade of what we see,
by what is countless and invisible.

( DAN BELLM, TRANSLATION )

Gabriel Fried

# THE MAJESTY OF PIERO DELLA FRANCESCA

In Monterchi, in August, I lament not being pregnant,
        not because I can't afford to pay
the token fee to stand inside the cool, dark chamber

before Piero della Francesca's *Madonna del Parto,*
        but because the gesture of waiving
that fee for the pregnant (as the sign outside

describes) is one I yearn to have extended to me.
        Never mind that I'm a man,
an assimilated Jew, and (perhaps most disqualifying)

an American tourist. It is in the nature of witnessing
        Piero's work to crave inclusion,
even as it is almost certainly withheld:

the two angels, mirroring each other at the tent-folds,
        could be completing an act of opening,
having spread the tent apart as the Madonna readies,

the graphic slit in her dress suggesting the imminence
        of a birth she seems poised
to perform herself—the long fingers of her right

hand already spreading the unfastened lips of fabric.
        For a moment before the illuminated fresco,
I am ecstatic at my improbable admission—

ecstatic that Piero's angels would anticipate, so
        many centuries in advance, the strength
of my agnostic hunger for transfiguration.

But then, creeping in, a doubt: To the Madonna's left,
        I can't help notice, one angel
(though, I'm told, an exact reflection of the other)

looks singularly ill from what, suddenly it seems,
        could only be my presence, his face sallow
with revulsion. And at that, even his twin, the picture

of heavenly health, seems indisputably at the brink
        of *closing* his half of the tent mouth,
when a heartbeat prior he had seemed to stake

my entrance to the birth of God.
        But this is Piero's majesty:
not the withdrawal of an invitation never

actually extended, not exclusion from the sacred.
        Rather, in his perfect depthless field rests
the static instant on which the impossible balances,

its flat, pregnant possibility infusing us. We, who
        otherwise might never know
the rapture of true communion, know it

in our unexpected longing. And if the curtain closes
        on my momentary grace,
it is not because I have been refused admission

to one viewing or another, but because
    I was granted transcendence for a spell,
momentarily forgetting the dimensions of my body.

Moira Egan
GRAVID

If pregnant women don't have to pay
the entrance fee, then what about me?
The Madonna del Parto gazes
(eyes inscrutable, fingers slitting
apertures in the celestial blue)
straight to my center of gravity.
Her two strange angels, each one-wingèd,
incomplete, grasp the heavy curtains:
opening, closing them, who's to say?

Long ago, a gypsy predicted
for me two daughters, one dark, one fair.
Grief and guilt come in colors, dull red,
queasy green. I said no to nature,
then nature turned and said no to me.
Frescoes pale with the passage of years,
or they chip and crack during earthquakes;
colors and lines grow ever less clear.
But this sinopia never fades.

Jorie Graham

SAN SEPOLCRO

In this blue light
        I can take you there,
snow having made me
        a world of bone
seen through to. This
        is my house,

my section of Etruscan
        wall, my neighbor's
lemontrees, and, just below
        the lower church,
the airplane factory.
        A rooster

crows all day from mist
        outside the walls.
There's milk on the air,
        ice on the oily
lemon skins. How clean
        the mind is,

holy grave. It is this girl
        by Piero
della Francesca, unbuttoning
        her blue dress,
her mantle of weather,
        to go into

labor. Come, we can go in.
    It is before
the birth of god. No one
    has risen yet
to the museums, to the assembly
    line—bodies

and wings—to the open air
    market. This is
what the living do: go in.
    It's a long way.
And the dress keeps opening
    from eternity

to privacy, quickening.
    Inside, at the heart,
is tragedy, the present moment
    forever stillborn,
but going in, each breath
    is a button

coming undone, something terribly
    nimble-fingered
finding all of the stops.

# Jane Hirshfield
## A COMMON COLD

A common cold, we say—
common, though it has encircled the globe
    seven times now handed traveler to traveler
    though it has seen the Wild Goose Pagoda in Xi'an
    seen Piero della Francesca's "Madonna del Parto" in Monterchi
    seen the emptied synagogues of Krasnogruda
    seen the since-burned souk of Aleppo

A common cold, we say—
common, though it is infinite and surely immortal
    common because it will almost never kill us
    and because it is shared among any who agree to or do not agree to
    and because it is unaristocratic
        reducing to redness both profiled and front-viewed noses
        reducing to coughing the once-articulate larynx
        reducing to unhappy sleepless turning the pillows of down,
            of wool, of straw, of foam, of kapok

A common cold, we say—
common because it is cloudy and changing and dulling
    because there are summer colds, winter colds, fall colds,
        colds of the spring
    because these are always called colds, however they differ
        beginning sore-throated
        beginning sniffling
        beginning a little tired or under the weather
        beginning with one single innocuous untitled sneeze
    because it is bane of usually eight days' duration
        and two or three boxes of tissues at most

The common cold, we say—
and wonder, when did it join us
when did it saunter into the Darwinian corridors of the human
do manatees catch them do parrots I do not think so
and who named it first, first described it, Imhotep, Asclepius,
    Zhongjing
and did they wonder, is it happy sharing our lives
    as generously as inexhaustibly as it shares its own
    virus dividing and changing while Piero's girl gazes still
        downward
    five centuries still waiting still pondering still undivided

while in front of her someone hunts through her opening pockets
    for tissues
                for more than one reason at once

# Karl Kirchwey
## MADONNA DEL PARTO

Now it is many years since I first saw her
          standing with one hand on her hip,
fingering the laces of her gown with the other,

a gown the color of Afghan lapis lazuli,
          in a gesture mixing impatience and eros,
or so it seemed to me, her swollen belly

split like fruit in an overwatered garden,
          but no sin in this for her, no sexual pleasure;
only that gaze, in chaste reproof cast down

at one so easily beset by panic:
          the child stopped eating because of the heat and dust
while we were on the road to Rome from Zürich;

the *passeggiata* outside our hotel window
          kept us awake, and when the morning came,
it seemed Love struck his tent and then withdrew.

She stands inside a fur-lined damask tent,
          and two angels, one wearing red, one green
(colors that go to make up a flesh tint)

in mirrored contrapposto move to drop
          the sides all figured over in pomegranates
on her impossible virginity, to keep

her from me, and her sacred calm, forever
        —or do they raise them instead, in their mercy,
that I might once more dwell in sight of her,

who have learned to keep a mortal trust with those
        I love, obliged like them to live in time,
as Piero made this work in seven days?

# G.Mend-Ooyo
## THE PREGNANT MADONNA

1
Rustling through the trees and their bushy branches,
the wind is returned with its ancient song.
The birds sing their songs among the new leaves.

2
Between the trees, grains thread their way across the fields.
The townsfolk of Monterchi are out sowing.
Each of the seeds is its own world.
They dream of growing, of spreading forth.

3
The countryside. A museum in a hill town.
The pregnantMadonna. The seed in her womb starts to move.
What sign does she sense in her palms?
Fifteenth century.
One step closer.
Twenty-first century.

4
Five centuries,
a single segment of time.
A single moment of time,
like an old acquaintance.
I feel Francesca's brush,
like a smiling woman, tickling my heart.
The angels would draw back the curtains of the years.
TheMadonnaenters for a single moment.
She draws back the curtain of pure white clouds
in the sky, as though removing her summer coat.

This is a moment before an amazing wonder.
This is the thought of all time.
It is the picture of the world before a rain of flowers
comes down upon the mountain peaks.
The pregnant Madonnais at hand.
And the world, my mother, is pregnant also.
   Madonna!

( SIMON WICKHAMSMITH, TRANSLATION )

Rickey Laurentiis
## SPEAK, BLOOD

But you couldn't see her darting past
Her beauty, running, a bird
The sound of red dust in the road . . .

Like you couldn't see my running
Against my own body, this one
That's been touched, entered, that moves

With this new communication in the blood.
So what is beauty? Here, in the present
Tense, post-diagnosis, post-reveal?

To be told, even by an angel, you must—
Your body must break to carry
This growing burden, if it is a burden.

If I cup my hand at my naked back,
Like her; if I can curve the other just right,
Just at the very crown of my stomach,

Like this, like her, so that the light,
The shadow, etcetera—Is that beauty?
Will I be seen cleanly again?

About a word: how it can stone a person,
Can show a life quite directly how it's already
Been changed—she is speaking that word

To me now, however too still she is,
Too calm, too white, but it's the lie that makes her
Beautiful, I think, like my lie: *I'm okay.*

# Honor Moore
## HER TENT, DAMASK OF POMEGRANATES

Her hair is tightly braided and encircling,
a crown but barely visible,
as if she has been asked to give over its force

to the unborn child within her belly
where her right hand rests, forefinger lifted.
Her gaze is lowered, reverent,

prescient of what we know lies ahead.
And then I notice her left arm bent at the elbow,
that hand on her hip, its fingers curling

away from the belly, as if the narrow space
behind her belonged as entirely to her
as the short past from which she has come.

See how she looks in two directions, right eye
toward the short life of her son as a boy,
his years as a man, when her own meaning

was subsumed into his. But now lift a hand,
obscure that eye, note her left side, girlish
hand on her hip, the eye insistent, giving lie

to all we believe we know, the rose
colored corner of her girlmouth edging up
as she becomes aware of the next moment.

SANSEPOLCRO

We see the figure of Christ rise up, horribly sylvan and almost bovine, a rustic form standing there like some fierce Umbrian peasant and contemplating from the edge of the sepulcher his acres of this world. —ROBERTO LONGHI

The best picture in the world.
—ALDOUS HUXLEY

*La Resurrezione (The Resurrected Christ)*

Rowan Williams
## RESURRECTION: BORGO SAN SEPOLCRO

Today it is time. Warm enough, finally
to ease the lids apart, the wax lips of a breaking bud
defeated by the steady push, hour after hour,
opening to show wet and dark, a tongue exploring,
an eye shrinking against the dawn. Light
like a fishing line draws its catch straight up,
then slackens for a second. The flat foot drops,
the shoulders sag. Here is the world again, well-known,
the dawn greeted in snoring dreams of a familiar
winter everyone prefers. So the black eyes
fixed half-open, start to search, ravenous,
imperative, they look for pits, for hollows where
their flood can be decanted, look
for rooms ready for commandeering, ready
to be defeated by the push, the green implacable
rising. So he pauses, gathering the strength
in his flat foot, as the perspective buckles under him,
and the dreamers lean dangerously inwards. Contained,
exhausted, hungry, death running off his limbs like drops
from a shower, gathering himself. We wait,
paralysed as if in dreams, for his spring.

# Franco Fortini
## SANSEPOLCRO

The thin wind hewing the gardens
rousing shadows of willow and thorn,
while wings and ice sharpen above ... Strong king
who smiles from the depths,
now turn your pupils to the cold
and look at me. You stare silent
and say now we've known it all.
And that death was true.
But the wind now delivers us unchanged and alive.
King, risen comrade, in me, a shawl at your throat,
your fists closed over your wounds,
let us go forth joined at the hip
amazed with gladness, talking of
the blue March beyond destiny.

( JONATHAN GALASSI, TRANSLATION )

# Karl Kirchwey
## A LIMBO OF VANITY

I

My life's so dark I must cover my eyes.
Whenever I am first in a new place,
   sleep itself is strange, and the body's postures
are inauthentic. After some time this goes,
   but the heart remains appalled at what it has
sought, which is change, when each day in its hours
   must be created new. Blood rises; gold dust rises:
a new day. I am in it now. I am in it always.

II
Rooster's cry or child's cry
    I cannot tell
what is going to wake me
    to the glistening foil
of light past the century-
    old umbrella
pine, or perhaps early
    traffic bound uphill

*Chicchirichi'*

    or a parish bell
Ineffably
    these mix their accents of base metal
beyond the almond tree
    whose blossom is celestial
against a rainy
    trunk, early and full

*Chicchirichi'*

But stiff denial
Wakes instantly
   And morning will
be desolate as that three-
    part brainless yell

*Chicchirichi'*

III
I am—slump. And catch myself.—Slump.
   It is so much easier to let go
than to feel the hot grain of awake.
   I got no sleep in the ditch of night,
on its gleaming edge of black.
   My root is quiet now.
I am sniffing roses in a Braille garden;
   This one is called "Lolita."
Persimmon peeled back; cinnamon.

       IV
       Here is a conundrum:
       what will kill Tiberius?
       A javelin pitched at a boar
       in the arena at Circeii;
          the squeal, the spurting blood;
       a muscle twisted in his side.

       See how that crown of palm
       tosses and catches the early
          light, each damasked blade

backswept and flickering.
   Powers move among us
which daylight has not yet colored;

  the rumour of thick night strung
mouths is that a god
   is coming from the East,
I am in love with marble sleep.
   My neck aches as if pillowed on
compacted sawdust,

   but I will appear to grope
only at first
   to find the trueing
edge of my disillusion.
   Even you do not surprise me—

V
And, dressed in rose, the Morning rises unsmiling
to avenge Himself on all the postures of dream.
That maimed tread, the great pivot of the hip: He is
about to step up, for once and all, and away,
thinking, How ever did they fashion a straight shaft
from this wood, from a seed placed in a dead man's
mouth? All it cries is, Give me more oblivion.

Steady yourself, Rider, with your unblinking gaze,
your thousand-meter stare. That night has been so long,
under its royal weight of law. Now smell the dew,
the coolness that lays the dust and blood for a while. Listen:

# Gjertrud Schnackenberg
## SOLDIER ASLEEP AT THE TOMB

In Palestine,
Where you are counting stars
To stay awake,
There is a legend that
The world was built
From nothing. There is a plaster crack
Ascending through the air
Above your head,
And you have laid aside
Your headgear
Covered with wolf skin,
But don't sink back,
Don't let your head
Tilt back, don't look up toward
The heaven's starry gulf and close your eyes,
Because you must not fall
Asleep. You must not sleep—
In Rome they crucified a dog
And carried it across
The city crucified upon its cross
Because once, long ago,
A dog in his old age
Slept through his watch,
And as he slept, the Gauls
Hoisted themselves in multiplying
Shadows across the brick
You lean your head on here—
You dream you run your palm across
A wall, and then, because
You must not fall asleep, you study it:

A map of enigmatic bricks
They manufactured in a city
Not located on the map,
With a thousand-thousand roads of mortar
Branching and rebranching
And, smiling from a pike
Before the gateway to the palace,
The head of a beheaded wolf
Tiberius once held up by the ears
And claimed was Rome,
Somehow become
A cap of wolf skin
You've retrieved
And laid in a sack
To carry on your shoulder,
Headed for Palestine—

You toil through mortar streets
Between the bricks
As if you knew the way,
But really you must admit
You're lost. But really
You must not lose the way.

As for that trench
Stretching before you
You dare not set your foot into that pit—
Rome is dried mud scattered into an opened
Artery. You must not drop away.
But then you do, you step away...
You step into a desert
Stretching out beyond

The outer city curb of Rome To Palestine,
Where you are counting stars
To stay awake,
Where a legend in this region says
The world was built from nothing,

But these colossal walls
Adorned with hoists and pulleys,
These wheels and ropes
Hanging from scaffoldings,
Transform the temple complex
Into siege towers they rolled up to the base
Of a wall where now you crumble
A little mortar in your palm,
No more than twenty grains,
Crushed out of lime, sand, straw, gravel,
Marveling as if it were all that was left
Of Rome—
Rome must have worn away
Behind this wall, buckled without a sound.
A bank of mud where someone
Plunged a torch and left a crater
Lit now by your torch,
A reservoir so vast an army drowns
Struggling to get across,
Racehorses floundering in shipwreck
Over flooded circus floors

Toward mass graves dug behind the Esquiline
For Pompey's elephants
Who pleaded for their lives,
For persecuted bears,

For waterspouts of birds
Slain on the sand floor of the arena
One piercing blue afternoon,
Now become merely a stench
Behind a supporting wall,

Though, like a room turned inside out,
The wall spills over,
A petrified waterfall
Of sludge from the ancient wars
They waged on animals,
And elephants are nudging you awake because
You must not sleep.
You lift your head. You are outside.
You cannot surrender
Your sense that there is still an outside
Outside.

But when you look out the corner
Of your eye, the heaps of
Flamingo carcasses the soldiers carry
On sagging litters,
As if they had done battle
With the sunset,
Become a heap of murdered angels
Pitchforked from a horrifying height.
You are afraid to look
To your right.
Outside, the world
Is a hurled object.
The world is a stone sphere
That has rolled through

Other lives, and as it grinds past,
It trails a red stream.
There is an atrocious
Implication here.
So you lower your head,
Keeping your eyes
Closed, as if that way nothing
Will be disclosed.
But you must not fall asleep,
Not even leaning on your shovel for a moment—

The world was built from nothing,
Not with the strewn
Abandoned trowels they used
For sealing off a crime,
Not with a general's
Unmentionable treasures
The soldiers were unloading
In a mountain range of spoils,
Not with mountains of lime,
Of sand, straw, gravel, while the god
Who made the world
Looked on in his foreboding—

But all through the empire
They built this same
Slipshod maze of rooms
Tilting on shallow foundations
You were digging
With a shovel
Below, in frightful terraces,
A brickwork complex hemmed in by

Several succeeding outer stairs
Rumored to lead outdoors
Just as you awoke because

You must not sleep, no matter what.
No matter how cold the nail
Embedded in the ice
Of three o'clock,
No matter who orders you to impale
The wolf's head you've been
Arrested with,
Alone, in man-made landscapes
Built with force, beneath
The creak of timber bridges,
And then that complicated falling down
Of nonexistent walls beneath
A watchtower whose foundation could
Equally have served
To hold a sanctuary up,

Where you take
A narrow hallway to the right,
Skirting the wall along a narrow passage
To reach the courtyard
Of—a palace like a marble mountain
In whose throne room you approach
Tiberius from behind his chair,
And he turns around—

There is an execution
At the heart of it.
Then several successive waves of terror,

As well as marble
From that island in the sea
Of Marmara, marble dust
Like the miraculous snowfall
In August delineating
The shape of the basilica:
A cruciform snowprint—
You lower yourself over the side,
To drop to the next terrace and run.

But each time you arrive here,
Lifting your lamp,
You hear a sound.
You know your orders, after all.
Yet when you put your eye
To a chink in the wall
And try not to inhale
The nauseating taste of mud

You see distant, underground
Fires pouring toward you
For miles and miles,
Underground walls buckling inward
On towering labyrinths,
And a native angel trundling
A dog he's saved
In a straw wagon with clattering
Wooden wheels,
A dog who gives a bark
And sticks his nose
Through the wooden slats
Against the angel's hand,

And cages of crucifixions, one by one,
Swaying above the heads
Of a group of distant soldiers;
But you step back,

You dream you run your palm
Across the wall, you dream
You guard an empty place
Where the plaster-crack ascending
Through the air above your face
Has multiplied,
As if a force behind the wall
Were pressing toward you
From the other side.

# Gjertrud Schnackenberg
## THE RESURRECTION

In the 1550s a lantern maker, Marco, testified
That as a child he had "led Piero by the hand"
Through the streets of Borgo San Sepolcro.
Piero, blind, and following a child guide along

The chessboard of his native city's streets
To the Civic Palace, within the tumbled walls
Of the Town of the Holy Sepulchre. Piero, blind—
Who once, with earth imported from the Black Sea,

Had dusted pinhole pricks on tracing sheets,
To trace *Dream of Constantine* on the wall,
And the serf who leaned against his shovel
Awaiting Helen's command to dig for the cross,

And Pilate, impassive, hooded in the Judgment Seat,
And the beautiful Jew who was tortured in a well—
Piero, white-gowned, a cataract prisoner, now
Shuffling, with outstretched hands, while far-off bales

Of straw, in fields ignited by the sunset,
Smolder behind him, setting a broken wall on fire.
The hem of a mantle of tree roots flames up
Like a patch of ancient sewing work littered

With those pearls for which Duke Federigo paid
A great price back in the old life, stitched
With silver leaf, in luminous embroiderings,
Lying tossed like a discarded shroud over

Kindling sticks in the hedge of thorns
The goldfinch once inhabited, her nest
A torch's head fallen from its stick
Beyond the curb of the marbly dream-town,

Where towers, knocked down across the countryside,
Half crumble like sugar-cube constructions
For a wedding, or dissolve like knocked-over
Buckets of sand for children's battlements,

For a city left behind in the wake of the earthquake
Of 1352, or the quake at Christ's death,
Since history is behind Piero now, and
The goldfinch is saved, circling ecstatically

Above Piero's head as he climbs a cement staircase
Step by step. *When you were young, you girded*
*Yourself and walked wherever you would. But*
*When you are old, you will stretch forth*

*Your hands and another will gird you,*
*And carry you where you would not go.*
Halting in the streets of Holy Sepulchre,
Grown old in the town of his nativity,

Taken by the hand to the Civic Palace,
He stops at the site of *The Resurrection,*
And lifts his outstretched hand from Marco's shoulder,
As if he groped for the lip of a stone coffin

From antiquity set only inches away from where
The blind man appears to be staring in fright
Into God's face. Behind him the pink twinkle
Of twilight is a banner moist with one drop

Of Jewish blood; before him, the distant
Blue mountain of Purgatory. His fingertips touch
Only picture-shadowing earth from the Black Sea.
Once he could squint at "The Resurrection" through

An ever smaller pinhole of light, like
A pinhole pecked for him by the finch's beak,
Through which he sifted powder for his drawings—
She whose nest had fallen when the mowers

Burned away the branches, she who had let
Piero approach, but only so far, and then
Warned him off with her gaze of terror,
When he would have bent on his knees in the grass

To stroke her anxious, silky head with
A fingertip, touching the scarlet cap
That stained it like a tiny, bloody drop,
But he'd backed away, not wanting to scare her—

But the pinhole he had peered through closed.
Now his shoes press against the plaster wall
Of blind old age, backed up by the empty place
Brick walls depict, where paint is a scent

That still could conjure the belfries of papier-mâché
He had painted for an important Duke,
A famous humanist he'd once depicted traveling
At twilight in a straw wagon with angels

Conversing in seraphic languages
Along the outskirts of a shining thunderstorm
Before the distant prospect of Rome-Jerusalem-Urbino.
Now he stands sightless with his empty hand

Outstretched at the rough edge of the sepulchre
Recently broken open, before which
Jesus has turned to Piero, holding out to him
Death's unraveled, pitiful bandages.

Monica Youn

# MARCH OF THE HANGED MEN

1

hyperarticulated giant black ants endlessly boiling out of a
heaped-up hole in the sand

2

such a flow of any other thing would mean abundance but these
ants replay a tape-loop vision

3

out of hell the hunger the thirst the righteous rage whose only end
is in destruction

4

the way the dead-eyed Christ in Piero's *Resurrection* will march
right over the sleeping soldiers

5

without pausing or lowering his gaze for he has no regard now for
human weakness

6

since that part of him boiled entirely away leaving only those
jointed automatic limbs

7

that will march forward until those bare immortal feet have
pounded a path through the earth

8

back down to hell because there is no stopping point for what is
infinite what cannot be destroyed

Piero's faces escape triviality because they are incarnations
of something beyond this world; or perhaps it is
beyondness itself that they seem so much a part of.
—MARK STRAND

Piero's St. Julian stares into the abyss of his future with
the forlornness of an already parentless child.
—JAMES R. BANKER

*San Giuliano (Saint Julian)*

Monica Youn

# PORTRAIT OF A HANGED MAN

the eyes / as if / pinned in / place tacked / up at
the corners / then pulled / taut then

pulled down / then endlessly / pouring down
the unstoppable / torrent from

the unseen / source as / if inexhaustible
downpouring remorseless / but made / of remorse

# Hélène Dorion
## THE FAULT

As if the page had been
torn, as if his body had worn away,
on the crumbling stone rests the face
of San Julian looking
into the distance at the scene where
covered in blood
his father and mother lie,
assessing the inevitable
destiny that imprisons us

—or is he looking, far into the distance
at the kindness rustling
in the ashes
the vast outline of our steps
that bring us back
to the beginning of history

—or, through the painter's eye, is he looking
at this fault that cuts through
every life at its core

( JONATHAN KAPLANSKY, TRANSLATION )

Mark Wunderlich
# FRAGMENT OF ST. JULIEN

The throat of the stag was never meant for speaking;
It would have pained the creature, to make the shapes,
to force the tongue and push against its single row of teeth,
make way for the warning to Julien, whose arrow
broke the bleeding hole the spirit of speech went in.
The first the beast spoke was warning, threat and pain
which is the way of all first language, the mouth
opening in surprise, the lungs seizing up to bark.
In the fragment of wall skimmed off and framed,
Julien too looks pained, regret not yet registered,
understanding leaking like a tint stirred into plaster,
his cloak still pulled around his shoulders, his club
gripped in his good hand, having beaten
the bodies of those who made him. Regret would come later
but for now he was more animal than that talking beast
who knew him for what he was.

AREZZO

A different fervor, grave and delicate, moves in the daylight of his pictures. Without our familiar passions, he is like a visitor to the earth, reflecting on distances, gravity and positions of essential forms.

—PHILIP GUSTON

*Mary Magdalene*

Mark Wunderlich

# PORTRAIT OF MARY MAGDALENE

On the road to Arezzo, the prostitutes
have set up their stations—a white plastic lawn chair
and a dusty spot with enough room for a driver
to pull over and inquire about the price. I suppose
they take their customers back into the woods
where an old mattress lies under a little roof of tin
and where the passing cars muffle the animal yelp
of a man's cum-cry. Meanwhile, in a church in town,
the rendition of the Magdalene stares down at us
from the Renaissance, but doesn't see, being nothing
but paint mixed into plaster. The artist has rendered her
with the soft lips and eyes of a farm girl, tented
her wide hips in pleats of green. He gave her
a cloak of red and white—partly thrown back,
partly pulled up to cover her new-found modesty,
her hair still wet from drying the feet
of a man who didn't want to hold her down
until he'd had enough, her face still dusty
from her station at the side of the road.
This is a portrait of kindness and contrition,
shame already fading as her hair begins to dry,
and this man takes her with him like a bride.
He is nowhere to be seen in the fresco—just her—
her seven demons already ground out into the dirt,
tossed like pots of night soil in the ditch.
On the road the women are still at work, cheap jewelry
catching a glint of the sun, high shoes improbable
for a walk into the woods, as one woman
casts down her cigarette and grinds
it's ember in the dirt. And where am I in all this?

A spectator thrilled or shocked a little,
my own demons still coursing through
the red riot of my veins, hidden
in the wet cave of my mouth like a man
I've caught in the back of my throat
until I spit his essence in the dust.
It is said Mary Magdalene boarded
a miraculous ship and rode it all the way to France.
There she died as a hermit in a cave
her hair grown long and gray. Her skull
can be seen there in a church. It's a holy thing,
this bony remnant, on which the contours
of flesh once formed a beloved face
though the reliquary preserves the decay.

Piero of the great mind, and the sweeping concept of the high regard for simplicity and the last reduction of emotion, glorious tact, superb rendering of the pause in rhythm, allowing no ridiculous effervescence or commonplace ebullience to over-ride his sense of measure, order, proportion and reality.    —MARSDEN HARTLEY

Possibly it is not a "picture" we see, but
the presence of a necessary and generous law.
—PHILIP GUSTON

*La leggenda della Vera Croce (The Story of the True Cross)*

Rebecca Okrent
PALIMPSESTS

As medieval scribes scraped Euclid from parchment
to ink in gilded doctrine and devotionals, so we scrape away
at unbelief to imprint ourselves with Piero's frescoes in Arezzo
where geometry was revived and a hodgepodge
of biblical heroics arrayed.
God is here,
above the courtyard where Mary,
interrupted from her reading, holds her place
while Gabriel annunciates.
But she will never return to her book or
life as lived before this moment,
cleaved onto plaster by Piero's brush.

There in a high lunette: the scene of Adam's death,
his children, stupefied, search each other's eyes
above a dreaming Constantine. If the face
looking out from Solomon's court is Piero's I,
afflicted with dumb history that repeats itself,
thank him for the triumph of mathematics and
the transports of his art.

Look now at Hericlius' bloodied battlefield. Blood seeps
out of a neck wound, splatters the horse's tail.     No.
The verbs are wrong. No one makes a move. I, too, am stilled.
The dagger-wielding, tender boys are harnessed by invisible lines,
Piero's code. All hell will break loose when he loosens his hold.

David Lehman

# THE LEGEND OF THE TRUE CROSS

1
On that July afternoon I went
to Arezzo to see the frescoes
by Piero della Francesca whom those
in the know called Piero and left it at that.

2
Where Adam died, a branch of the forbidden tree
grows and she worships it and he chops it down
and there you see the marital destiny
of the human race.

3
Who died on it, who died because of it.
The cross replaces the shield
as knights brandish swords
on the battlefield.

4
The angel wakes the emperor
and shows him a cross of white stars in the sky.

5
The knife is an iron cross with a blade.
And thus, with the blowing of a horn,
the legend of the true cross was born.

Pier Paolo Pasolini

*from* RICHES

He takes a few steps, raising his chin,
but as though a hand were pressing
down on his head. And in that naïve,
labored pose, he holds still, granted entry
inside these walls, into a light
he fears, as if, unworthy soul,
he had troubled its purity...
Under the crumbling base he turns
his tiny head, his shaven
workman's jowls. And into vaults aflame
above the half-light through which he passes
as though flushed from a den, he casts
suspicious animal glances; then, ashamed
of his boldness, he briefly turns his burning eyes
on us; then looks back up again... Again
the sun blazes pure in the vaults
from an invisible horizon...
Breaths of flame from the stained glass to the west
color the wall, and those eyes
look on in fear, surrounded by people
well versed in such things; but he does not kneel
in the church, does not bow his head—and yet
so pious in his wonder, in the waves
of daylight, at the figures
another light breathes into the space.

Those limbs of the demon-possessed, those dark
backs, that chaos of green soldiers
and violet horses, the pure
light veiling everything

in shades of fine dust: it's havoc,
it's butchery. The humbled gaze distinguishes
bridle from sash, forelock from mane,
the light blue arm raised to cut a man's throat
from the brown one bent to parry the blow,
the horse stubbornly backpedaling
from the horse, upended, kicking
hard into the bleeding throng.

Yet already the eye, bewildered, looks
down, turns elsewhere ... Bewildered it comes
to rest on a wall where it discovers,
suspended like two world, two bodies ... one
in front of the other, in an Asian
penumbra ... a dark-haired youth,
limber in his bulky clothes, and she,
she, the innocent mother, matron unfledged,
Mary. Those lowly eyes recognize her
at once. But, meek in their impotence,
they do not brighten. And it's not the sunset
blazing in the sleepy hills of Arezzo
that veils them ... It's a light
—oh, no less sweet than this,
surely, but supreme—shed
by a cloistered sun where Man became God,
now shining on this humble hour of prayer.

And shining, below,
on the hour of first sleep, in the young
and starless night enfolding Constantine
and emanating from an earth
whose warmth is an enchanted silence.

The wind has abated, while a few
of its dying breaths wander as though
lifeless through thickets of motionless hazels.
Perhaps with mournful vehemence the insects'
joyous wheezing rasps in gusts inside
the open tent, amid voices unsleeping, perhaps,
and some vague ballads with guitars . . .
Yet here, over the milky, raised curtain,
the apex, the unadorned interior,
there is only the darkening color
of sleep, as in his camp bed
like a white humpbacked hill
lies the emperor, whose peaceful, dreaming form
reflects the fearsome peace of God.

                    *

Froth are the eyes that slavishly
fight this Peace and, by now resigned,
squint to see if it's time
yet to leave, if the bustle here
and its muffled hum will take him back
to everyday life and the cheerful
noises of evening. Froth the bands
of bourgeois behind the crumbling altar,
shielding their eyes with their hands,
stretching their tired faces,
overcome by a thirst
(which transcends them and sends them
rushing after other testimonials) to bear
faithful witness to a past that is theirs.

Froth—under San Francesco's
bricks already black, on cobblestones
a distant sun drowns in a light
now hopelessly colorless—
the weary sounds of parking lots
and half-empty cafes . . .
Froth, though hotter, indeed
happier, the ferment
of all this life, lost and all too beautiful
when rediscovered here so fleetingly,
desperately, in a land
that is only vision . . .
In the square, inside the circle of Trecento
houses, a din of children's voices hangs
in air, the only sound: if you look around,
you'll count no less than a thousand of them,
sons of the provinces, with their little faces
and their prudish shorts; and as the rods and planks
of grandstands for the Palio
have turned the piazza into a kind of cage,
they now swarm and flit about,
their murmur running riot in the evening,
a frantic flock of little birds . . .

Ah, outside, a time of pious country
evenings returns, while inside,
old wounds of nostalgia reopen!
These are places, lost in the rural
heart of Italy, where good and evil
still mean something, as the fervor
of youngsters froths in innocence,
and the young men are virile

in souls offended, not exalted,
by the mortifying test
of sex, the ordinary
wickedness of the world. And if,
full of honesty ancient as the soul,
the men here keep believing
in some kind of faith—
and the humble fervor of their acts so grips them
that they lose themselves in a commotion without memory—
then higher still, and more poetic
Is this froth of life.
And blinder the sensual regret
not to be what others feel, than ancient drunkenness.

(STEVEN SARTORELLI, TRANSLATION)

## Charles Wright

## WITH EDDIE AND NANCY IN AREZZO
## AT THE CAFFÉ GRANDE


Piero in wraps, the True Cross *sotto restauro*,
Piazza desolate edge
Where sunlight breaks it,
                              desolate edge
Where sunlight pries it apart.
A child kicks a soccer ball. Another heads it back.

The Fleeting World, Po Chu-I says, short-hops a long dream,
No matter if one is young or old—
The pain of what is present never comes to an end,
Lightline moving inexorably
West to east across the stones,
                              Cutting the children first, then cutting us.

Under the archways, back and forth among the tables,
The blind ticket seller taps and slides.
*Lotteria di Foligno, Lotteria di Foligno,*
                              He intones,
Saturday, mid-May, cloud bolls high cotton in the Tuscan sky,
One life is all we're entitled to, but it's enough.

Why is Piero della Francesca so
different from other quattrocento artists?
The longer one contemplates his work, the more imperative
that question becomes. It haunts the viewer...
—WALTER KAISER

Anyone who studies his frescos in Arezzo cannot
fail to feel his charm, his sincerity, and
the truly decorative character of his painting...
—RUSSELL COWLES

*L'Annunciazione (The Annunciation)*

Rick Barot
## THE AREZZO ANNUNCIATION

It is not always joy
        that is announced to you
in the mundane light.

Not always a wing
        or a flood of new knowledge

delivering its atoms of change
to your body.
        Sometimes it is

a wound delivered,
just as plainly as in this
        painting, her face closing

into itself, into an angle
        of understood responsibility.

No fanfare in the room
other than some structure inside
        made flat

by what you have received,
        the heart a putty-colored

folding chair knocked
to the ground.
        And the room itself emptied,

this is part of the recognition.
                    The room a wound,
                    the light a wing on the floor,

the atoms of dust
                    in the shaft. And the quiet,
that is grief's appetite.

Because many viewers of the frescoes knew the narrative, Piero sought to multiply visual significance beyond the story, thereby engaging the viewer on several levels and stimulating participation and contemplation. —JAMES R. BANKER

The quiet chant of the air and the immense planes are like a choir against which Piero's dramatic personae remain silent. —ZBIGNIEW HERBERT.

*La Morte di Adamo (The Death of Adam)*

# Henri Cole
## ADAM DYING

Though the most we can say is that it is
*as if* there was a world before Adam,
Even that seems narrow and parochial
as we contemplate his dying . . . While Eve,
with withered breasts, watches pensively,
and the mellifluous young, in animal skins
stand about emotionless, like pottery.
What do the significant glances mean?

Can only Adam—naked, decrepit,
sprawled in the dirt—see what dying is?
How can they not hear the moaning, smell the body,
suffer the burden of original sin?
East & West, armies revile each other.
Mothers hunt among the decomposing dead.

The initial appearance of the cross in Piero's cycle is remarkably understated. In the nocturnal Vision of Constantine on the bottom tier of the back wall, an angel swoops down like a magnificent bird, its bright radiance striking the front of the red and gold tent and the counterposed soldiers in the foreground.

—JERYLDENE M. WOOD

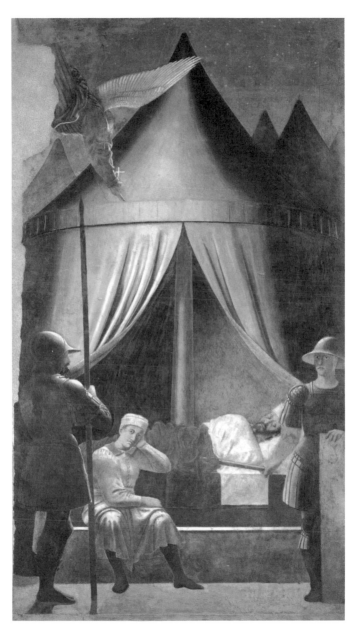

*Sogno di Costantino (The Dream of Constantine)*

James Brasfield

# EARLY AFTERNOON, HAVING JUST LEFT THE CHAPEL OF SAN FRANCESCO

Radiant the delayed calmness,
—Do you feel it, I said.—Yes, you said,

of what only each can know,
kernel of radiance, the *globo terrestre*

of a water drop, not the passing adaptations
of canonical light, but seconds stilled—

our hearts beating through the moments—centuries
of the next tick of a watch relieved,

a world enough in time to imagine
Piero walk to work across cobblestones

toward a completion, his close attention
to sunlight passing through shadows

owned by the sharp angles of buildings,
sunrays warming what they touch

Piero, first a painter, is not a monk.
He will make what welcomes light

a source of light: slow the day
he will add lucent black wings

to white feathers of the magpie
ever alight on a roof-edge.

I found a feather on a stone, feather I thought
from the angel's wing, that arc of light

held aloft in descent, shared with us
and Constantine in his dream.

I think of a white egret returning home near
the high creek, through unwavering

evening light, to sleep, sleep at Sansepolcro,
where we were headed in a rental car.

# Gjertrud Schnackenberg
## THE DREAM OF CONSTANTINE

Long after the Messiah's men have entered
Every room in the city, and long after
Your government and seat of earthly power

Trudges far to the north, its army tents recentered
And sunk, like a meteor burned into the map,
This is the real end of the Roman Empire,

This storyless, this never-heard-of place
You find within, where there is only Constantine,
And vegetation, nudging the faces of the boulders

*. . . you saw rivers washing the very gates of the towns,*
*from the bend which leads the highway back toward Belgica,*
*you saw everything waste, uncultivated, neglected, silent,*

*shadowy—even military roads so broken that scarcely*
*half-filled, sometimes empty wagons cross them . . .*
*You gave us your whole life . . .*

And there is a letter fallen out of the sky—
Through a window, far off in the distance
They have drawn the dripping body of Maxentius

From the river and fixed his head on a pike,
To send it to Africa—but you dream an alphabet letter
Would shine beyond the borders of the New Rome, except

You had your men pry out and melt the bronze,
Leaving a chasm in the shape of a lightning-obliterated
Monogram, and there will come a time as well that,

Once you have laid your hands on the treasure
Of the nails that fastened His hands,
You will melt them into bridle bits and a helmet

And precious coins stamped with your portrait.
A letter fallen, a chunk of pediment, a stone
Carved from the fallen fragments of a dead moon

That turns out, when you examine it, to be
A meteor fragment with an engraved, ambiguous
Pockmark among other stoned plunged into walled gardens

An empress studies in a miniature, circular
Hand mirror she holds over her shoulder, studying
Her hair, and the void at the heart of power

Where the senators don't speak Latin anymore,
Where barbarian horses clatter the cavalry stairs—
But when she turns around to look, Rome isn't there,

Only marble-carved studies of leaf-and-shadow
Floating above the entrance to gates
Long thought to be the handiwork of Greek slaves,

Crowned with orange blossom, and senators convene
To share their thoughts and turn to you,
But when you look through the gate you see

Nameless prisoners milling in a pig yard—
You lay down a law that the sacred precinct
May not be violated. No one may approach

The plot of ground you set aside, an orchard
Painted with bird cages for the Empress
And nightingales in flight and fountain jets

Raining parabolas of evaporating silver.
But as you approach, you see a figure
Strung up by the neck in the afterlife

Above the jawbone of an ass, clothes shredded,
While in the background, Christ is beaten and bound.
*The secret of the Empire was now disclosed:*

*That an emperor could be made elsewhere*
*Than at Rome.* Other planets. Other laws.
Other hammers knock an alabaster sheet

Into a maze of cracks, a map of conquered districts,
New countries for the levying of the tax;
Other shovels are striking at an urn marked,

In the simplest imperial style, simply "Bones."
Your bones, Constantine, for in the end nothing
Could save you. But as for one's death, fixed into

The future like a stone that cries out in a wall,
It isn't now in any case, not at this moment.
There are churches to build, with spirits drawing

Compass points in the dust only steps ahead
Of Constantine, and letters to write to Jerusalem:
*We wish this church to be the most beautiful in the world.*

*We have issued instructions to that effect*
*To the Vicarius Orientis, and the Governor of Palestine.*
You awaken, in a tent on a field of battle.

Though your men boil grass to drink the water,
Though the moon flickers out—the battle is over
Long after the Messiah's men have entered

Every room in the city, and long after
Your engineers have affixed a pentacle
To the city and reported rumors of its miraculous

Founding, long after the dedicatory mosaic,
The visual liturgy, the setting for a crisis
In gold glass, monophysite particles swimming upward

Out of the prisons of ecclesiastical geography,
Escaping when everything must be included,
Escaping when nothing must escape, not even dust,

For history is either a prison, a repository belonging
To the victorious Emperor, or else a patch of snow
A group of kneeling slaves hammers and hammers—

Let them hammer the heads of their own shadows.
You will win the battle. The city of Rome is yours,
And never mind the rumors thronging your ears

Like angels pouring along a map of black roads
Through the mosaic's gold squares, angels rushing
Toward you through the labyrinths of mortar

From other capitals with other crucifixions
At the ends of other lanes, dimly beheld
In cities that have yet to be founded,

At whose outskirts other emperors sleep in their tents.
For now there is you at the picture's center.
And never mind the angels thronging your cars

With rumors of lamps up ahead that refuse
To stay lit for your armies, with rumors
That no lamps are lit in the cities your armies enter.

# Patti Smith
## CONSTANTINE'S DREAM

In Arezzo I dreamed a dream
Of Saint Francis who kneeled and prayed
For the birds and the beasts and all humankind.
All through the night I felt drawn in by him
And I heard him call
Like a distant hymn

I retreated from the silence of my room
Stepping down the ancient stones washed with dawn
And entered the basilica that bore his name
Seeing his effigy I bowed my head
And my racing heart I gave to him I kneeled and prayed
And the sleep that I could not find in the night
I found through him
I saw before me the world of his world
The bright fields, the birds in abundance
All of nature of which he sang
Singing of him
All the beauty that surrounded him as he walked
His nature that was nature itself
And I heard him—I heard him speak
And the birds sang sweetly
And the wolves licked his feet.

(O Signore, fa' che sia strumento della tua Pace:
Dove c'è odio, lascia che sia Amore.
Dove c'è offesa, Perdono.
Dove c'è dubbio, Fede.
Dove c'è disperazione, Speranza.
Dove c'è oscurità, Luce.

Dove c'è tristezza, Gioia.
fa' ch'io non cerchi tanto
di essere consolato, quanto consolare.
di essere compreso, quanto comprendere.
di essere amato, quanto amare.)

But I could not give myself to him
I felt another call from the basilica itself
The call of art—the call of man
And the beauty of the material drew me away
And I awoke, and beheld upon the wall
The dream of Constantine
The handiwork of Piero della Francesca
Who had stood where I stood
With his brush stroked The Legend of the True Cross
He envisioned Constantine advancing to greet the enemy
But as he was passing the river
An unaccustomed fear gripped his bowels
An anticipation so overwhelming that it manifested in waves

All through the night a dream drew toward him
As an advancing Crusade
He slept in his tent on the battlefield
While his men stood guard
And an angel awoke him
Constantine within his dream awoke
And his men saw a light pass over the face of the King
The troubled King
And the angel came and showed to him
The sign of the true cross in heaven
And upon it was written

In this sign shall thou conquer

In the distance the tents of his army were lit by moonlight
But another kind of radiance lit the face of Constantine
And in the morning light
The artist, seeing his work was done
Saw that it was good

In this sign shall thou conquer

He let his brush drop and passed into a sleep of his own
And he dreamed of Constantine carrying into battle in his right hand
An immaculate, undefiled single white Cross
Piero della Francesca, as his brush stroked the wall
Was filled with a torpor
And fell into a dream of his own

From the geometry of his heart he mapped it out
He saw the King rise, fitted with armor
Set upon a white horse
An immaculate cross in his right hand.
He advanced toward the enemy
And the symmetry, the perfection of his mathematics
Caused the scattering of the enemy
Agitated, broken, they fled

And Piero della Francesca waking, cried out
All is art—all is future!
Oh Lord let me die on the back of adventure
With a brush and an eye full of light
But as he advanced in age
The light was shorn from his eyes

And blinded, he laid upon his bed
On an October morning 1492, and whispered
Oh Lord let me die on the back of adventure
Oh Lord let me die on the back of adventure

And a world away—a world away
On three great ships
Adventure itself as if to answer
Pulling into the New World
And as far as his eyes could see
No longer blind
All of nature unspoiled—beautiful—beautiful
In such a manner that would have lifted the heart of St. Francis
Into the realm of universal love

Columbus stepped foot on the New World
And witnessed beauty unspoiled
All the delights given by God
As if an Eden itself, as if Eden had opened her heart to him
And opened her dress
And all of her fruit gave to him
And Columbus so overwhelmed
Fell into a sleep of his own
All the world in his sleep
All of the beauty, all of the beauty entwined with the future
The twenty-first century
Advancing like the angel
Advancing like the angel
that had come
To Constantine
Constantine in his dream
Oh this is your cross to bear

Oh Lord Oh Lord let me deliver
Hallowed adventure to all mankind
In the future
Oh art cried the painter
Oh art—Oh art—cried the angel
Art the great material gift of man
Art that hath denied
The humble pleas of St. Francis
Oh thou Artist
All shall crumble into dust
Oh thou navigator
The terrible end of man
This is your gift to mankind
This is your cross to bear
And Columbus saw all of nature aflame
The apocalyptic night
And the dream of the troubled King
Dissolved into light

MILANO

Great art—lifelines to the unseen, aspiring to the primitive and to the mysterious at once, may emerge from Piero's epiphanies. His paintings synthesize form and content, substance and spirit.

—ANNE B. BARRIAULT

He was perhaps the first to use effects of light for their direct tonic or subduing and soothing qualities.

—BERNARD BERENSON

*Pala di Brera (Madonna and Saints)*

# Antonella Anedda
## OVAL MEMORY

Almond of light circling the memory
in a book thicker than the one we opened together
our love that seemed so slow and yet was only a hint
like the egg in the scallop shell in the painting
of the oval-faced Madonna seated
within the oval circle of saints.

( SARAH ARVIO, TRANSLATION )

URBINO

In her nature she is, briefly, monumental, as are those miraculous specimens of the human race, the nurses of kings.

—ROBERTO LONGHI

*Madonna di Senigallia (The Madonna of Senigallia)*

# Massimo Gezzi

## LOOKING AT THE MADONNA OF SENIGALLIA

The swath of light that hits
the dark wall behind the Virgin
and lights it up—you can decipher its outline,
the swirling motes that Lucretius sang.
And the stone's embrace, the warmth
that one might feel if only
he would turn and brush against it,
that spot of sun.
it must have been briny,
that air so bright, so
masterfully stolen by Piero
for his sacred theme: beyond the shutters, outside,
you sense a marina dazzled by light,
the same as now, as this clear windy
January sky with the grooms
taking care of the horses, the leather of the shoes
clacking on the cobblestones, and he (not here: in a semi-
lighted room) who sees that swath and understands
that that's the only thing that can speak the truth of the world,
and he with his careful brush does not ignore it,
he makes it real.

( DAMIANO ABENI AND MOIRA EGAN, TRANSLATION )

A certain anxiety persists in the painting of Piero della Francesca. What we see is the wonder of what it is that is being seen. Perhaps it is the anxiety of painting itself.

—PHILIP GUSTON

*La Flagellazione (The Flagellation)*

# Henri Cole
## THE FLAGELLATION

Soon they'll knock nails into him, but first there's this,
a lesson in perspective with two worlds coming together:
one gloomy and transgressive, let's call it super-real,
a world behind this world, in which a man is tied to
a column—his hair and beard unkempt, his body raw,
though not bleeding—muttering, "I am afraid to fall down,
but I will not be dominated"; the other world is surreally
calm, with saturated colors and costumes of the day,
a youth's head framed by a laurel tree, nothing
appearing larger than it is, so the eyes drift back
to the deviant, the melancholic, the real, emotion
punching through the rational—like mother cat with five
kittens in her tummy purring in my lap now—
as a man for his beliefs receives blow after blow.

# THE PIERO TRAIL AND OTHER THOUGHTS

I am attracted to (Piero) by his intellectual power: by his capacity for unaffectedly making the grand and noble gesture, by his pride in whatever is splendid in humanity. And in the artist I am peculiarly sympathetic to the lover of solidity, the painter of smooth curving surfaces, the composer who builds with masses.

—ALDOUS HUXLEY

When we travel, otherness has two senses: we're obviously "the other," but the world we encounter is also "the other."
—EWA HRYNIEWICZ-YARBROUGH

PIERO DELLA FRANC. PIT.
DAL BORGO A S. SEPOL.

# Albert Goldbarth

# 1400

Saps, and the anal grease of an otter, and pig's blood,
and the crushed-up bulbous bodies of those insects
that they'd find so quickly gathered on barnyard excrement
it makes a pulsing rind, and oven soot, and the oil
that forms in a flask of urine and rotting horseflesh,
and the white of an egg, and charcoal, and the secret
watery substance in an egg, and spit-in-charcoal
in a sluggish runnel of gray they mixed
with the harvested scum of a bloated tomato,
and steamed plant marrows beaten to a paste,
and orange clay, and auburn clay, and clay bespangled
with the liquid pearl of fish scales stirred in milt,
and suet, and glue boiled out of a hoof,
and ash, and grape-like clusters of fat grabbed
out of a chicken carcass and dried in the sun
until it became inert and yet still pliable, and lime,
and the pulp of the cherry, and the pulp of the cherry
immersed in egg, and coral in a powder,
and silver flake, and fig, and pollen, and dust, and beeswax,
and an iridescence scraped with infinite care
from the wings of hundreds of tiny flying things,
and salted iridescence, and human milk, and ores,
and gall, and stains expressed from teas, and gobs of squeeze-off
from the nettings of cheese, and rouge, and kohl,
and luster, and oyster, and lees: and so from these
they made their paints: and then
their Gods and their saints.

Dave King
THE TRAIL

It was the view, of course, the high piazza
ornamented by its stairs. The town
a handsome crumple on its slope, the rise
of sudden trumpets toward the view. Oh air,
oh town that opens singing, like a bellows.

Or else it was the soup. More than that soup,
of course, more than the nights the soup evoked.
The noise of rain outside, promise of other
rains and suns (a bus ride to the sea),
sudden invitations, wine and olives.

It was the art. Of course it was the art!
In love with curves, a painter conjures circles,
curve on curve, the sockets of the eyes,
round horses' haunches, thighs as plump as loaves.
We love the form and seek the form in love.

It is ineffable. Not just the sum
of days recalled and days traversed and days
quickly forgotten (those days, of course, the days
we trust we'll harvest most, if blindly).
Air: unknowable except as art.

It wasn't sad, for one thing. Out of gray
there's blue, and joy is bonded to the plaster,
to the blue. Great swinging curves and bony
sunlight, distant silverware. Of course
it was the pleasure. The pleasure was all ours.

Jacqueline Osherow

# VIEWS OF LA LEGGENDA DELLA VERA CROCE

How will I ever get this in a poem,
When all I have to do is type AREZZO
And the name sidles up along a station platform,

The train I'm riding in begins to slow,
And—though I swore I wasn't getting off this time—
I know a train comes every hour or so

To wherever I'm headed—Perugia? Rome?—
And suddenly I'm rushing off the train,
Depositing my bag, crossing the waiting room,

And striding up the Via Monaco again
As if I couldn't see each fresco perfectly,
Couldn't see them, now, against this screen....

But in a minute, they'll array themselves in front of me:
Soldiers, horses, placid ladies, kings,
All patient, in their places, not spinning crazily

Like the first time I saw them: unearthly beings
Breathing luminous pearl-green instead of air,
Horses and ladies-in-waiting flapping wings

Stolen from the eagle on the soldiers' banner,
Their brocaded sleeves and bridles grazing spinning walls,
Hat twirling, armor flying, coils of hair

Unraveling into whirling manes and tails—
And that was before the winged arm's appearance. . . .
When the *Times* ran an article about Stendhal's

Famous nervous breakdown from the art in Florence,
Half a dozen friends sent it to me.
I suppose these tales of mine require forbearance.

Not that I had a breakdown, though I was dizzy,
Closed my eyes, leaned against a wall,
And told myself that there was time to see

Each panel—one by one—down to each detail:
Hats, sleeves, daggers, saddles, bits of lace;
I studied every panel: *Adam's Burial,*

*St. Helena's Discovery of the Cross,*
*Solomon Meeting Sheba, The Annunciation,*
*The Dream of Constantine, The Torture of Judas,*

Whose other name I learned from a machine
Which, with the help of a hundred-lire coin,
Supplies a telephone with information.

I did it for a laugh; I chose Italian.
I thought I heard *the torture of the Jew*
And was so stunned I played the thing again

(My Italian was, after all, fairly new
And the woman on the tape spoke very quickly
But she did say *the torture of the Jew*—

In Italian it's *ebreo*—quite matter-of-factly)
*The torture of the Jew who wouldn't reveal*
*The location of the true cross*—I got it exactly—

Put in a lot of coins to catch each syllable
(I also heard the English, which said *Judas*),
All the while not looking at the rope, the well;

Instead, I chose a saintly woman's dress,
An angel's finger pointing to a dream,
A single riveting, incongruous face—

What was I supposed to do? They were sublime.
The Inquisition wasn't exactly news
And, while I did keep my eyes off that one frame,

I wasn't about to give up on those frescoes.
In fact, I saw them again, a short while after
And again soon after—in those heady days,

Trains cost almost nothing and a drifter
Could easily cover quite a bit of Italy,
Though I tended to stay in Tuscany. The light was softer,

And—probably not coincidentally—
It had a higher density than any other place
Of things that could dazzle inexhaustibly.

And I was insatiable, avaricious
For what—even asleep—a person can't see
From a slim back bedroom in a semidetached house

Like every other house in its vicinity
On a site whose inhabitants had been wiped out
To make room for spillover, like my family,

From the very continent I would have dreamed about
If I'd had even an inkling of the mastery
Of what its subtlest inhabitants had wrought

When they weren't doing away with people like me....
See how Solomon, listening, leans his head?
How the tired horseman leans against a tree—

How the guard beside the emperor's makeshift bed
Can't resist the sorcery of sleep—
So only we can catch the angel's finger pointed

At the dreamer's head, the horse's sudden leap,
As if straight from that vision, to the battle scene:
Christianity's triumph over Europe....

I love the wing, the arm, the dreaming Constantine,
The moonlight casting shadows on the tent—
It *is* moonlight, though there is no moon—

Pale, as always, silvery and slant;
It's coming from the angel's pointing arm
Which I didn't even notice that first moment—

All I saw was undiluted dream—
I didn't really care what it was for—
Besides, we fared no better under pagan Rome,

Which hadn't stopped me from going there—
I might not even have thought about Jerusalem,
If I hadn't found myself staring straight at her.

I was wandering lazily around the Forum
Without even a guidebook or a map.
I didn't care which stones were the gymnasium,

Which pillars hunched together, needing propping up,
Paid tribute to which boastful, scheming god.
Amazing, I suppose, that all that stuff could keep—

The advantage of stone, I guess, over mud and wood—
But the things I like best are always beautiful;
I don't admire antiquities as I should,

I lack the imagination for them. Still,
In my own haphazard way, I was thorough;
I did cover everything, though I'd had my fill,

Walked through every arch, every portico,
And—there—in the middle of the Roman Forum
Was my own first menorah, stolen years ago,

My altar, carved with rams' horns on its rim
(If you want to find them, they're on the Arch of Titus,
On your right, as you face the Colosseum;

*Splendid reliefs*, the *Blue Guide* says;
It's the only arch acknowledged with a star)—
Soldiers were parading them, victorious,

Transporting them—if only I knew where. . . .
What was I doing at these celebrations,
When I'd fasted over this, year after year,

Chanting the entire book of Lamentations
In candlelight, sitting on the floor?
*How she's become as a widow, that was great among nations. . . .*

The torture of the Jew couldn't compare.
After all, wasn't it a work of fiction?
This was actual footage from a war

Which had always been—forgive me—an abstraction,
Despite—or because of?—all the people killed
Trying to save the Temple from destruction,

The few survivors forced to watch as every field
Around Jerusalem was plowed with salt,
Then brought to Rome in chains, for all I knew to build

This very chronicle of their defeat.
Still, if you take the long view, here I am
And Titus isn't anywhere in sight.

Besides, I'd hate to sacrifice a ram
Or whatever's required—bullock, turtledove—
I much prefer the chance to chant a psalm

When I need a quick, relatively foolproof, salve
Or have managed to entangle myself yet again
In a muddle only God would ever forgive.

(Like this breeziness about the Temple's destruction,
This complete inability to feel its loss,
Not to mention my ridiculous and total passion

For Piero's *Legend of the True Cross*,
The way Jerusalem is most alive to me
When it looks just like Arezzo in his frescoes.)

It's not a matter of faith—though it should be—
But the chance to infiltrate with my own voice
All that unadulterated majesty.

Don't be too shocked, I'm often blasphemous;
It's a deal I have with God; at least I pray.
Though He may have a plan—I'm not impervious—

In which I'm expected to wake up one day,
Go to synagogue, recite the psalms,
And convince myself with every word I say.

Beggars can't be choosers; these are godless times;
Let Him hold on to His illusions.
Besides, maybe I do have a few qualms

About my persistent heretical allusions
To Someone who is—after all—a Deity. . . .
You'll find I'm a jumble of confusions.

Besides, I'm not sure God much cares for piety;
My guess is—since David was His favorite—
That He's partial to passion, spontaneity,

And likes a little genuine regret.
True, David lost his ill-begotten child—
But what did the pious ever get?

Unless you buy that dictum in the Talmud
That the reward for the commandment is the commandment—
In which case, nothing's ever withheld,

But that may not be what the rabbis meant.
And who am I, at the end of a mangled century,
To talk about God, reward, and punishment?

Especially from this vantage point, in Italy—
And that's where we are, gaping, in Arezzo—
Though there are lots of places we could be:

Florence, Santa Maria Novella, the piazza
Where they rounded up the Jews to ship them east. . . .
Or reading some *well-known facts* about matzoh

In a just-published newspaper in Bucharest
(How it must contain the blood of Christian children);
Or even at a swim meet, as Europe's finest

Actually do a synchronized routine
About the Nazis and the Jews and win the cup.
Why not Ostia Antica, in the ruin

Of the oldest known synagogue in Europe?
Go yourself, take the Rome Metro, *Linea B*;
Otherwise, you'll think I'm making this up.

They found it building a road in 1960.
At first it looks like any Roman basilica:
Columns with ornate capitals, a stairway,

And then you notice bits of Judaica
On some of the columns—*lulav, etrog, shofar*—
And, after a while, looking down, the swastika

Patterned in the black-and-white mosaic floor—
I know, I know, it was an obvious design:
Bold, easy to lay out; you see it everywhere—

But to me, it's a harrowing premonition:
We should never have set foot on such a continent;
How could we have failed to see this omen,

Which, even in retrospect, will not look innocent
Of what it would inevitably mean?
As if no Jewish building on the continent—

Not even under layers of earth—escaped that sign,
But, still, it's third century (let's call it C.E.
Since *my* Lord is, after all, an older one)

And there—carved in the marble, for all to see—
Are a few of my most beloved eccentricities:
The *shofar*, with its desperate cacophony,

And the *etrog* and *lulav*—pure frivolities
Of gathered citron, willow, myrtle, palm,
Shaken in the air to jumbled melodies

Of a congregation belting out a psalm,
Then circling the room chanting hosanna
Call it piety. Call it delirium—

Citron, willow, myrtle, palm, hosanna—
No one's even certain what they mean,
Unless it's sheer loveliness, sheer stamina—

Some say the citron's a heart, the palm branch, spine,
The willow leaf's two lips, the myrtle, eye
(Does every group of plants concoct a human?)

But this came after the commandment—some rabbi,
Improvising, finding similarities,
But I say God devised it purely whimsically—

*(And ye shall take you . . . the fruit of goodly trees,*
*Branches of palm trees, and the boughs of thick*
*Trees and willows of the brook),* merely to tease

The solemn air in which they were to frolic. . . .
Maybe God prefers synagogues as I do:
Dismantled, as in Ostia, bucolic,

A few columns and mosaics in a meadow,
The grass and weeds so high you think you're lost.
He can slip out, that way, incommunicado;

One day in seven isn't enough rest.
Not that I claim to understand His ways—
I'd fail, if He put me to a test

Of anything but willingness to praise—
But still, I would think the UJA
Or World Jewish Congress would be able to raise

Enough funds to pave a little pathway
From the rest of Ostia Antica to the synagogue . . .
For older people, for instance, it's a long way

(Since, as usual, the local Roman demagogue
Banned synagogues within the city wall)
And some of them might be cheered to see an *etrog*,

A *lulav*, a *shofar* on an ancient capital,
The way, when I'm standing on the *bimah*,
Chanting ancient columns from a scroll

And come to, say, *They called the place Be'er Sheva*
*And so we call it to this very day,*
I feel a kind of wild reverse amnesia,

Having forgotten—and suddenly remembered—all eternity,
Proof, beneath my narrow silver pointer,
That there will be no end to this very day . . .

But I'm forgetting the swastikas on the floor,
The distance from town, the torture of the Jew,
The roundup in Florence, the Judean war,

Who Italy's allies were in World War II
Before their final-hour about-face,
How—if you make your way to Urbino,

To enter the double turrets of the palace
That looks like something Piero once dreamed up
To house his enigmatic masterpiece

(*The Flagellation*, the reason for your trip)—
You will also have to forget the Paolo Uccello.
Or walk right by it. Don't even stop.

Don't let the helpful guide attempt to show
The beauty of its composition, frame by frame,
How the tiny golden circle that appears to glow

Between the stately woman's finger and thumb
Is the sacred host—stolen from the altar—
Purchased by a Jew for a hefty sum;

How the red stream, in the next frame, on the floor
Is blood from the host burning in his fireplace
As soldiers with spears and axes throng his door.

One child sobs, one grabs his mother's dress;
The blood has seeped outside, through stone and mortar
And into the next frame's version of the stateliness

Of a clerical procession to the altar:
Incense. Psalter. Cross. *The Host Returned*.
Next, the woman, out in a field somewhere,

Is met by an angel and . . . what? forgiven? warned?
Before the soldiers hang her from a tree . . .
Then the Jew, with wife and children, is burned;

The flames near one child's head, the other's knee
(All four are tied together to the stake).
But we don't see the Christian woman die;

In the final frame she's on a catafalque,
A pair of devils grabbing at her feet
For what the angels, at her head, will not forsake

Without at least putting up a fight.
(My money's on the angels, but it's close.)
The guide calls it Uccello's greatest insight

To leave us with something so ambiguous—
A spiritual struggle . . . iniquity.
You see, I didn't heed my own advice;

I actually asked the guide to tell the story,
And a crowd gathered round to listen in.
No one blinked an eyelash but me . . .

Perhaps they didn't notice the children
Burning, in that fifth frame, at the stake. . . .
It is, after all, a nighttime scene;

The Jew is wearing red, the children, black.
Besides, in Europe, burning Jewish children
Aren't all that difficult to overlook,

What with the complex struggle over sin
And so much never-ending beauty—
And even I, who see them, still take in

The two Pieros, the Raphael, the ideal city
Which unreal Urbino still resembles . . .
Is there anything more despicable than ambiguity?

How could I not have left the palace in shambles?
Or, at least, burned the painting publicly?
I'm not interested in symbols

With two breathing boys right in front of me
Burning with their parents on a palace wall
For anyone who comes along to see

Or, rather, not see—since they're invisible
To all but specially trained eyes.
Tie a rope around me. Throw me in a well;

I'm sick of this unnatural disguise.
Sick of turning away. Sick of everything.
I need—as in Arezzo—to close my eyes,

To stop these flames and likenesses from spinning
From the painted to the identical real landscape,
But it's worse with my eyes closed; now they're careening

Around my tight-shut eyelids' burning map—
That red you get when you shut your eyes in sunlight
Consuming the entire extent of Europe—

A continent notoriously profligate
Of knees, heads, fingers, elbows, thighs.
Wasn't *this* Uccello's greatest insight:

That if you gradually habituate the eyes
They will be capable of watching anything?
I wonder if this came to God as a surprise.

Could He actually have known about this failing
And still gone ahead with our creation?
You can't, after all, have everything;

We're pretty good at visual representation,
Not to mention all those people who could sing
And care for sheep while arguing with a vision. . . .

He's certainly done His share of watching
And nonetheless managed to survive.
Unless He hasn't. But I'm not touching

That one. Besides, when you work out how to live
Your one puny life on this unnerving earth,
It's so much more appealing to believe

In some strategic artistry, some worth,
As if bitterness were a fleeting misconception.
I do have a fondness for the truth

But am willing to make, in this case, an exception,
Which has been, more or less, my people's way.
We've learned to be remarkable at self-deception

What with the Messiah's long delay. . .
Just look at the Jew in the fresco in Arezzo,
Why have I avoided him until today?

Clearly he's faking it—the first Marrano
(According to the legend he's accepting Jesus)—
That's not how rapture looks to Piero;

The over-the-top bliss is preposterous.
The Jew was probably desperate to get dry. . . .
He hasn't got a clue about the location of the cross;

He can't even manage his own inventory.
Where's his holy ark? his candelabrum?
Why are these bits of ash dredging the sky?

Where's his citron, willow, myrtle, palm?
What's that splinter in his upturned eye?

## Allison Seay
## THE WIDE BLUE AIR

A white moth in San Sepolcro. Outside the church, I stood on the
cobblestones and the beautiful woman wearing the yellow scarf
told a story: the streets were made by hand the width of one man's
reach. A man on his knees laying down a city stone by stone.
Inside but hidden, (invisible) artifacts: milk from the Virgin, a lock
of her hair, Christ's blood, his foreskin. And then, the new roses in
bloom—Jude the Obscure—and lemon trees. A bloom even before
the fruit smells as delicious as the fruit itself.

Charles Wright
UMBRIAN DREAMS


Nothing is flat-lit and tabula rasaed in Charlottesville,
Umbrian sackcloth,
                    stigmata and *Stabat mater*,
A sleep and a death away,
Night, and a sleep and a death away—
Light's frost-fired and Byzantine here,
                              aureate, beehived,
Falling in Heraclitean streams
Through my neighbor's maple trees.
There's nothing medieval and two-dimensional in our town,
October in full drag, Mycenaean masked and golden lobed.

Like Yeats, however, I dream of a mythic body,
Feathered and white, a landscape
                        horizoned and honed as an anchorite.
(Iacopo, hear me out, St. Francis, have you a word for me?)
Umbrian lightfall, lambent and ichorous, mists through my days,
As though a wound, somewhere and luminous,
                              flickered and went out,
Flickered, and went back out—
So weightless the light, so stretched and pained,
It seems to ooze, and then not ooze, down from that one hurt.
You doubt it? Look. Put your finger there. No, there. You see?

# Notes on the Poets and Translators

DAMIANO ABENI (b.1956), an Italian epidemiologist, began translating American poetry in 1973 when on a scholarship in the United States. An honorary citizen of Tuscan, Arizona, he lives in Rome.

ANTONELLA ANEDDA (b.1955), from Rome, Italy, is the author of numerous books and libretti, including the poetry collections *Residenza invernali*, which won the Sinisgalli Prize, the Diego Valeri Prize, and il Tratto Poetry Prize; and *Notte di pace occidentale*, which won the Eugenio Montale Prize.

SARAH ARVIO (b.1954) is an American poet, essayist, and translator, the author of three poetry collections. She has received a Guggenheim Fellowship and a National Endowment for the Arts Translation Fellowship.

RICK BAROT (b.1969) was born in the Philippines and raised in the San Francisco bay area. He is the author of two books of poetry and is a professor at Pacific Lutheran University in Seattle.

JUDITH BAUMEL (b.1956) is a professor and director of the MFA program in creative writing at Adelphi University. The author of three books of poetry, she is a poet, critic and translator living in the Bronx, New York.

DAN BELLM (b.1952) is a writer, editor, and translator from Berkeley, California. He has published three books of poetry and won fellowships from the National Endowment for the Arts, and the California Arts Council.

JAMES BRASFIELD (b.1952), twice a Senior Fulbright Fellow to Ukraine, is the author of two collections of poetry and a book of translations. He has received fellowships from the National Endowment for the Arts and the Pennsylvania Council on the Arts, as well as the PEN Award for Poetry in Translation.

HENRI COLE (b.1956) was born in Japan and raised in Virginia. The author of nine poetry collections, he is the former Executive Director of the Academy of American Poets and has won the Berlin Prize, the Rome Prize, and the Amy Lowell Poetry Traveling Scholarship.

Hélène Dorion (b.1958) is a Canadian poet. She has published over twenty books of poetry and fifteen artists' books.

Moira Egan (b.) is an American poet and translator living in Rome. She is the author of *Cleave, La Seta della Cravatta/The silk of the Tie,* and *Spin.*

Jorge Esquinca (b.1957) is the author of fifteen books, most recently the poetry collections *Descripción de un brillo azul cobalto / Description of a Flash of Cobalt Blue,* translated by Dan Bellm, and *Cámara nupcial,* along with the book of essays, *Breve catálogo de fuerzas.* He lives in a village at the shore of Lake Chapala, Mexico.

Franco Fortini (1917–1994) was an Italian poet, journalist and intellectual, as well as a translator of the writing of Brecht, Flaubert, Gide, Goethe, Kakfa, Proust, and many others.

Gabriel Fried (b.1974) is an editor and teacher, and the author of *Making the New Lamb,* a collection of poems.

Jonathan Galassi (b.1949), President of Farrar, Straus, and Giroux in New York, is a poet and novelist, and a translator from the Italian of poetry by Giacomo Leopardi, Primo Levi, Eugenio Montale, and others.

Massimo Gezzi (b.1976) is a poet and writer from the Marche region of Italy. He is a founder of 'le parole e le cose' and has been an Italian Fellow at the American Academy in Rome.

Albert Goldbarth (b.1948) has published over 25 collections of poetry and has received fellowships from the National Endowment for the Arts and the Guggenheim Foundation.

Jorie Graham (b.1950), an American poet, was raised in Rome, Italy. She has been awarded a MacArthur Fellowship, the Morton Dauwen Zabel Award from the American Academy and Institute of Arts and Letters, and the Pulitzer Prize for *Dream of the Unified Field: Selected Popems, 1974–1994.* She is the Boylston Professor of Rhetoric and Oratory at Harvard University.

Jane Hirshfield (b.1953) has published seven books of poetry, and has received numerous awards, among them a Guggenheim Fellowship, a National Endowment for the Arts fellowship, and the Donald Hall–Jane Kenyon Award in American Poetry. She is a Chancellor of the Academy of American Poets.

Jonathan Kaplansky (b.1960) has translated works by Hélèn Dorion, Annie Ernaux, Hélen Rioux, and others. He currently lives in Montreal.

Dave King (b.1955) is the author of the novel *The Ha-Ha*, which won the 2006 Rome Prize.

Karl Kirchwey (b.1956) is a Fellow of the American Academy in Rome, where he also served as Andrew Heiskell Arts Director. In addition to his poetry, his work includes book reviews, translations, literary curatorship, and advocacy for writers and writing.

Rickey Laurentiis (b.1989) is the author of a poetry collection, *Boy with Thorn*, which won the 2014 Cave Canem Poetry Prize.

David Lehman (b.1948) is the author of many acclaimed books of poetry and nonfiction, and the founder and series editor of the *Best American Poetry* series. He worked as a journalist for many years and teaches at the New School University.

G.Mend-Ooyo (b.1952) is President of the Mongolian Academy of Culture and Poetry. He was raised by a nomadic family and began writing poetry at age 13. He has published over 40 books of poetry, which have been translated into 40 different languages.

Honor Moore (b.1945) is the author of three poetry collections and two works of nonfiction, including *The Bishop's Daughter: A Memoir*, a *Los Angeles Times* Favorite Nonfiction Book of 2008, a *New York Times Book Review* Editor's Choice, and a National Book Critics Circle Award finalist.

Rebecca Okrent (b.1950) is author of *Boys of My Youth,* a collection of poems.

Jacqueline Osherow (b.1956) is the author of seven poetry collections. She has won the Witter Bynner Prize and fellowships from the Guggenheim Foundation, the National Endowment for the Arts, and the Ingram Merrill Foundation.

Pier Paolo Pasolini (1922–1975) was an Italian film director, poet, writer, and intellectual. He wrote his first poetry when he was seven years old and continued through his writing and film to explore Italian life, dialects, religion, social constructs, and politics.

Steven Sartarelli (b.1954) is a translator from French and Italian into English. He has translated Andrea Camilleri's popular detective novels as well as the works of Bufalino, Roberto Calasso, Casanova, and Pier Paolo Passolini.

Gjertrud Schnackenberg (b.1953) has won numerous awards for her five collections of poetry, including the Los Angeles Times Book Award and the Griffin International Poetry Prize. She is also a recipient of the Rome Prize from the American Academy in Rome and the Berlin Prize from the American Academy in Berlin.

Allison Seay (b.1980) is the author of *To See the Queen*, winner of the 2012 Lexi Rudnitsky First Book Prize in Poetry.

Patti Smith (b.1946), a frequent traveler to Italy, is an American singer-songwriter, poet and visual artist, a vital part of the NYC punk rock movement of the 1970s. She is a Commander of the Ordre des Arts et des Lettres of the French Ministry of Culture and in 2007 she was inducted into the Rock and Roll Hall of Fame. She won the National Book Award in 2010 for her memoir, *Just Kids*.

Simon Wickham-Smith (b.1968) is a British musician, academic, translator, and astrologer. He is director of the Mongolian Academy of Poetry and Culture and the Danzanravjaa Foundation, and co-director of the Orchuulga Foundation, an organization dedicated to the translation of Mongolian literature. He is currently a lecturer at Rutgers University.

Rowan Williams (b.1950) is an Anglican bishop, theologian, scholar, teacher, and poet, and a Fellow of the British Academy. He currently serves as the 104thArchbishop of Canterbury.

Charles Wright (b.1935), poet laureate of the United States, was born in Pickwick Dam, Tennessee. While stationed in Italy with the Army he began to read and write poetry. He received the National Book Award in 1983 and the Pulitzer Prize in 1998 and serves as the Souder Family Professor of English at the University of Virginia in Charlottesville.

Mark Wunderlich (b.1968), the author of three poetry collection, has received the Lambda Literary Award for Gay Men's poetry and the Rilke Prize. He is a Professor of Literature at Bennington College in Vermont.

MONICA YOUN (b.1971) is an American poet, trained as an attorney, who was raised in Houston, Texas. She is the author of three collections of poetry, *Barter*, *Ignatz*, which was a finalist for the National Book Award, and *Blackacre*.

# Acknowledgments

Many thanks to Gabriel Fried and Persea Books, to the Board of the Civitella Ranieri Foundation for sabbatical time to work on this collection, and to my colleagues at Civitella and at the American Academy in Rome, where I served as Andrew Heiskell Arts Director for five years.

With Sarah Kozlowski (my art historian niece), I pulled together an initial Piero handbook of essays, poems, maps, and research while both employed at the Academy. I am indebted to Sarah for such excellent collaboration, as I am to my son, Jacob, and husband, Don, with whom I have spent countless hours visiting the Pieros. They were my best possible company in developing this book. I want to thank, too, Catia Agnolucci, Akiko Busch, Caren Canier, Curt Collins, Frank DaBell, The Feltus family, Jonathan Galassi, Margaret Kuntz, Marcia Hall, Jean McGarry, Diego Mencaroni, Honor Moore, Jane Oliensis, Ingrid Rowland, Trude Schnackenberg, and Tina Summerlin for all of their various encouragement and assistance with this book. And thank you, Mark Strand, dear missed friend.

To all the contributors, you amazing poets: *grazie mille.*

*

Thanks to the following publishers, authors, estates, and translators for their permission to reprint the poems in this book, as indicated:

Antonella Anedda: "Oval Memory," translation copyright © 2016 by Sarah Arvio. Reprinted by permission Donzelli editore (Rome) and the translator.

Rick Barot: "The Arezzo Annunciation," copyright © 2016. Reprinted by permission of the author.

Judith Baumel: "World without End," copyright © 2016. Reprinted by permission of the author.

James Brasfield: "Early Afternoon Having Just Left the Chapel of San Francesco," copyright © 2016. Reprinted by permission of the author.

Henri Cole: "Adam Dying" from *Pierce the Skin: Selected Poems 1982–2007* by Henri Cole. Copyright © 2010 by Henri Cole. "The Flagellation" from *Touch* by Henri Cole. Copyright © 2011 by Henri Cole. Reprinted by permission of Farrar, Straus and Giroux, LLC.

Hélène Dorion: "The Fault," translated by Jonathan Kaplansky. Translation copyright © 2016. Reprinted by permission of the author and translator.

Moira Egan: "Gravid," copyright © 2016. Reprinted by permission of the author.

Jorge Esquinca: "Nostalghia," translated by Dan Bellm. Translation copyright © 2016. Reprinted by permission of the author and translator.

Franco Fortini: "Sansepolcro," translated by Jonathan Galassi. Translation copyright © 2016. Reprinted by permission of Jonathan Galassi and the heirs of Franco Fortini.

Gabriel Fried: "The Majesty of Piero della Francesca," copyright © 2016. Reprinted by permission of the author.

Massimo Gezzi: "Looking at the Madonna of Senigallia," translated by Damiano Abeni and Moira Egan. Translation copyright © 2016. Reprinted by permission of the author and transator.

Albert Goldbarth: "1400" from *To Be Read in 500 Years.* Copyright © 2008 by Albert Goldbarth. Reprinted with the permission of The Permission Company, Inc., on behalf of Graywolf Press, Minneapolis, www.graywolfpress.org.

Jorie Graham: "San Sepulcro" from *Erosion* by Jorie Graham. Copyright © 1983. Republished with permission of Princeton University Press. Permission conveyed through Copyright Clearance Center, Inc.

Jane Hirshfield: "A Common Cold" from *The Beauty* by Jane Hirshfield. Copyright © 2015 by Jane Hirshfield. Reprinted by permission of Alfred A. Knopf, an imprint of the Knopf, Doubleday Publishing Group, a division of Random House, LLC. All rights reserved.

Dave King: "The Trail," copyright © 2016. Reprinted by permission of the author.

Karl Kirchwey: "Madonna del Parto" originally appeared in *A Limbo of Vanity*, a publication of the American Academy in Rome. Copyright © 2016. Reprinted by permission of the author.

David Lehman: "The Afternoon of the True Cross," copyright © 2016. Reprinted by permission of the author.

Rickey Laurentiis: "Speak, Blood," copyright © 2016. Reprinted by permission of the author.

G.Mend-Ooyo: "The Pregnant Madonna," translated by Simon Wickhamsmith. Translation copyright © 2016. Reprinted by permission of the author and translator.

Honor Moore: "Her Tent, Damask of Pomegranates," copyright © 2016. Reprinted with permission of the author.

Rebecca Okrent: "Palimpsests," copyright © 2016. Reprinted by permission of the author.

Jacqueline Osherow: "Views of *La Leggenda della Vera Croce*" from *Dead Man's Praise*, copyright © 1999 by Jacqueline Osherow. Used by permission of Grove/Atlantic, Inc.

Pier Paolo Pasolini: "The Riches" from *The Selected Poetry of Pier Paolo Pasolini: A Bilingual Edition*, translated by Steven Sartarelli. Translation copyright © 2014 by Steven Sartarelli. Reprinted by permission of the University of Chicago Press.

Gjertrud Schnackenberg: "The Dream of Constantine," "The Resurrection," and "Soldier Asleep at the Tomb" from *Supernatural Love: Poems 1976–1992* by Gjertrud Schnackenberg. Copyright © 2000 by Gjertrud Schnackenberg. Reprinted by permission of Farrar, Straus and Giroux, LLC.

Allison Seay: "The Wide Blue Air," copyright © 2016. Reprinted by permission of the author.

Patti Smith: "Constantine's Dream" "Constantine's Dream" © 2016 by Patti Smith. Reprinted by permission of the author.

Charles Wright: "Umbrian Dreams" and "With Eddie and Nancy in Arezzo at the Caffé Grande" from *Negative Blue: Selected Later Poems* by Charles Wright. Copyright © 2000 by Charles Wright. Reprinted by permission of Farrar, Straus and Giroux, LLC.

Mark Wunderlich: "Fragment of St. Julien" and "Portrait of Mary Magdalene," copyright © 2016. Reprinted by permission of the author.

Monica Youn: "March of the Hanged Men" and "Portrait of a Hanged Man," copyright © 2016. Reprinted by permission of the author.

*

Thanks to the following rights-holders for permission to reproduce the photographs of the paintings of Piero della Francesca included in this book.

*Madonna del parto*. Photo credit: Nicolo Orsi Battaglini / Art Resource, NY

*The Resurrected Christ*. Photo credit: Scala / Art Resource, NY

*Saint Julian.* Photo credit: Scala / Art Resource, NY

*Mary Magdalene.* Photo credit: Scala / Art Resesource, NY

*The Story of the True Cross,* "Battle of Constantine and Maxentius." Photo credit: Scala/Ministero per i Beni e le Attività culturali / Art Resource, NY

*The Story of the True Cross,* "The Annunciation". Photo credit: Scala/Ministero per i Beni e le Attività culturali / Art Resource, NY

*The Story of the True Cross,* "The Death of Adam". Photo credit: Scala/Ministero per i Beni e le Attività culturali / Art Resource, NY

*The Story of the True Cross,* "The Dream of Constantine". Photo credit: Scala/Ministero per i Beni e le Attività culturali / Art Resource, NY

*The Madonna of Senigallia.* Photo credit: Nimatallah / Art Resource, NY

*The Flagellation.* Photo credit: Scala/Ministero per i Beni e le Attività culturali / Art Resource, NY

*Madonna and Saints.* Photo credit: Alfredo Dagli Orti / The Art Archive at Art Resource, NY